Richard Beauchamp

Medieval England's Greatest Knight

Richard Beauchamp

Medieval England's Greatest Knight

David Brindley

TEMPUS

First published 2001

PUBLISHED IN THE UNITED KINGDOM BY:

Tempus Publishing Ltd
The Mill, Brimscombe Port
Stroud, Gloucestershire GL5 2QG

PUBLISHED IN THE UNITED STATES OF AMERICA BY:

Tempus Publishing Inc.
2 Cumberland Street
Charleston, SC 29401
(Tel: 1-888-313-2665)

Tempus books are available in France, Germany and Belgium
from the following addresses:

Tempus Publishing Group	Tempus Publishing Group	Tempus Publishing Group
21 Avenue de la République	Gustav-Adolf-Straße 3	Place de L'Alma 4/5
37300 Joué-lès-Tours	99084 Erfurt	1200 Brussels
FRANCE	GERMANY	BELGIUM

British Library Cataloguing in Publication Data.
A catalogue record for this book is available from the British Library.

ISBN 0 7524 1970 6

Typesetting and origination by Tempus Publishing.
PRINTED AND BOUND IN GREAT BRITAIN.

Contents

Preface

My fascination with Richard Beauchamp grew because almost every day for the last six years I have looked at his effigy in the beautiful chapel which was built by his executors in fulfilment of his will. A three-month sabbatical in 2000 gave me the opportunity of researching his life, and this book is the result of that time.

Many people have helped me in the preparation of this book. I am grateful to the staff at Warwick Records Office and in the British Library Manuscripts Room for their help and guidance. Thanks to Doreen Mills who took some of the photographs of the Beauchamp Chapel and Thomas Beauchamp. Noel Reeve generously allowed me to use her cottage in Devon which gave me the space and peace to write. Trevor Barr accompanied me on a research trip to Normandy, following in Richard's footsteps.

My daughter Catherine helped with some translations from Latin, and my son Matthew made many stylistic suggestions. My daughter Rachel helped with researching Shakespeare's portrayal of Beauchamp.

This book is dedicated with love to Gill, my wife, in the year of our Silver Wedding Anniversary.

Acknowledgements

Colour plates 1-18 and 23 are from the author's collection. All other illustrative material is drawn from the Tempus Archive.

Introduction

The closing centuries of medieval England were a time of great contrasts, and Richard Beauchamp was a child of his age. He has been described as 'an avaricious knight errant with a taste for the spectacular,'[1] and as 'one of the few honest and upright figures in these difficult years'.[2] The contrasts exhibited by the closing years of the middle ages begin to look like complex contradictions when they are seen through the life of an individual.

It was an age when the arts and crafts of architecture, painted glass and illuminated manuscript reached their highest achievements; it was also an age when the plague brought obsession with death and piles of bodies were seen in the cities. There was a deep-seated fear of hell and there was naïve joy in simple pleasures. There were elaborate pageants and magnificent feasts; yet chronic debt and economic depression meant that villages were left depopulated and overgrown. Methods of torture were devised to prolong the agony of a prisoner while keeping him just alive; Christian piety was at its height, with Mary and the Saints being elaborately venerated. Ladies were cosseted and treated with dignified respect; witches were hunted down and burned at the stake. The great castles and Churches were a riot of colour and pattern; most people lived in drab single-room hovels.

The fifteenth century was not only a time of startling contrasts; it was also a century which saw an acceleration of great change sweeping across Europe and leading to a new era. Chivalry had been a common way of life binding the aristocracy and knights in a single code of purpose, behaviour and honour; but the rise in national identity and new methods of warfare such as the development of the cannon meant that this code was drawing its last breath. Handwritten books, richly illustrated and illuminated, were among the greatest treasures produced by European culture, but printing was about to be invented. Schools of copiers would no longer be needed and books, once an expensive luxury owned by few outside the monasteries, would be widely available. Feudalism had provided an economic and social system in which the strata of society all had a clear position and knew their duties; but the authority of lord, state and Church was becoming open to question and challenge. All of them were to change radically within the span of a few decades.

Richard Beauchamp was one of the richest of medieval figures (a recent article in *The Sunday Times* placed him eighth in a list of the two hundred richest people in history). Within a generation, however, his great fortune was to be split and then to disappear, for he was the last male of his line to reach adulthood. He was fêted as one of the greatest medieval knights, developing an international reputation for his ability in jousting and as a military commander. He was, perhaps, the last great medieval knight, for the age which he represented was rapidly passing. The values that dominated Richard's life were on the way out. The united crown of England and France which he fought all his life to establish was a lost cause by the time of his death; fighting with lances and bows and arrows was fast being superseded by modern technology.

Those who have seen George Bernard Shaw's *St Joan* or Shakespeare's history plays of the first half of the fifteenth century, *Henry IV, V* and *VI*, will already have a view of the sort of person Richard Beauchamp was. Shaw portrays the earl of Warwick as ruthless and single-minded in his determination to have Joan executed. For Shakespeare he appears little more than a cipher – a loyal, perhaps plodding, courtier on the fringes of power. Neither playwright approaches the reality of Richard Beauchamp, and Shakespeare continually confuses him with his son-in-law Richard Neville, 'the Kingmaker'. To be fair to the dramatists, however, it is notoriously difficult to write the biography of a medieval figure.

We are fortunate that there is a large amount of contemporary documentary evidence about Richard Beauchamp. There are household records from Warwick, Rouen and Berkeley castles from periods when he was living in them; there are Privy Council minutes of meetings at which he was present; there are eye-witness accounts of sieges and battles in which he took part; there is a unique pictorial biography following his career from birth to death. All these add up to give a detailed picture of his campaigns, estates and travels. It is often possible to pinpoint exactly where Richard was, what he was doing, and even what he had to eat on particular days for months at a time. It is surprising, then, that there is no adequate biography of him.

For the modern reader, however, the most interesting parts of a human life are not so easily discovered about a person who lived six centuries ago. Motivation – the underlying psychological force of a personality – was not an issue raised by the medieval mind. Richard was conventionally portrayed as loyal, courageous, honourable and religious. How he was affected by his father's imprisonment; whether he felt conflict between his Christian devotion and his brutality in war; his interaction with his family and close associates –all these can only be guessed at, although at times there are certainly strong hints and indications in the material. What we can be certain of is that conflict was a determining factor in his development as an adolescent and young adult. He and his family were at the centre of the intrigue which brought the Lancastrian dynasty to the English throne and kept it there for sixty years. Richard was also part of the very small group of people who, with Henry V, defeated France between 1415 and 1420, and then lost it again under Henry VI.

Richard was, then, a great soldier and diplomat. He was also an extraordinarily able businessman, heading an empire with a private civil service that would make modern international companies look insignificant. Moreover, he was a patron of the arts and illuminated manuscripts, history books, and music commissioned by him still survive. We even have a poem written by Beauchamp to his second wife, one of the richest medieval heiresses and a member of the Spencer family that produced Diana, Princess of Wales. His main artistic legacy is the chapel specified in his will and built on to St Mary's Warwick after his death. It is 'one of the few buildings in England that can still give us an impression of medieval religious feeling, and show the importance of all the arts in giving it expression.'[3]

Medieval art, military strategy, politics, religious faith, business management and social structure were all interdependent, despite the great contrasts and contradictions found in the age. Unlike the twentieth and twenty-first centuries, life was seen as all of a piece. Coming to understand Richard Beauchamp, then, will give us an insight into his times.

1

The Beauchamps of Warwick

The Beauchamps were perhaps the most consistently successful family among the English nobility for a period approaching two centuries. They acquired the title of earl of Warwick by good fortune rather than by judgement, and managed to hang on to it by producing a male heir who grew to adulthood in each generation – an achievement equalled by very few other aristocratic families in an age when infant mortality was high. Between the years 1268 and 1445 there were six Beauchamp earls of Warwick, and in each generation, with only two relatively minor setbacks, the family increased its wealth and influence by involvement in war, good marriages, and consistent royal and political service. During these closing centuries of the middle ages, there was almost no major military expedition in which an earl of Warwick was not present and playing a significant part. From the border struggles with Scotland and Wales to the battlefields of France at least four of the six highly distinguished themselves, and two of them – the first Earl Thomas and Richard himself – were among the greatest military commanders of late medieval times.

The century from about 1340 to 1440 was dominated by three themes. The Black Death, which swept across Europe to kill about one third of the population of England around 1350, brought devastation which was to blight the economy for several generations. Fresh outbreaks of the plague were liable to occur at any time, although none of them approached that of the mid-fourteenth century in severity. With the population decimated, labour was scarce; land owned by the Beauchamps produced decreasing income as the fourteenth century entered its second half, although they countered this by adding to their holdings.

The second major development was the longbow, and its contribution to the 'Hundred Years' War'. At Crécy and Agincourt, and at other set-piece battles, its skilled use gave the English a clear advantage over the French who were using the much slower crossbow and were encumbered by excessive body-armour. The Hundred Years' War also brought economic problems for England – the monarchy was rarely out of debt for the duration of the hostilities. For individual commanders such as a Beauchamp, however, great riches were to be reaped, and the family profited greatly from their campaigns in France.

The third dominant theme was the rise of religious and political dissent, the first stirrings of the storm which at the beginning of the sixteenth century was to become the Reformation. The heresy trial of Wycliffe in 1384, the Lollard rebellions which gathered pace across Europe in the early fifteenth century, and the 'Peasants' Revolt' of 1381 were all indications that the Church and the aristocracy no longer had an unbreakable grip on the minds and actions of the king's subjects. Individual conscience was beginning to assert its strength; tradition and authority began to look as thought they might be open to question.

The Beauchamps had been hereditary sheriffs of Worcestershire since Norman times, when a Walter Beauchamp married the daughter of Urse d'Abitot, William the Conqueror's notorious and brutal sheriff of Worcestershire, around 1110. Where the name originated is unknown, but the small village of Beauchamps a few miles south of the River Somme is the strongest candidate. For more than a century, the family gathered a useful, but by no means outstanding, range of estates in Worcestershire, the centre of their operations being Elmley Castle near Evesham. Their first major piece of good fortune happened in 1268 when William Beauchamp inherited the title of earl of Warwick through a convoluted series of marriages, deaths and failures of the male line. The focus of the Beauchamps' interest began to shift from Worcestershire to Warwick, although the family were to retain a close attachment to the Worcestershire manors, with Elmley and Hanley Castles and Salwarpe, near Droitwich, all featuring significantly in the subsequent family history.

Little information survives about William, who remained as earl of Warwick until his death in 1298. He fought a number of times against the Welsh between 1277 and 1294, and was involved in a campaign on the Scottish borders in 1294. It is likely that at some stage he went on pilgrimage to the Holy Land as the three crosslets which he added to the family coat of arms were generally an indication of this act of piety. Of his character all that we know is that he had a reputation for hot-headed behaviour. On hearing a rumour that someone else had been buried in place of his father, he dug up the grave in the Church of Friars Minor in Worcestershire and exhumed the corpse. He was excommunicated for sacrilege.[4]

William's most important contribution to the Beauchamp family, besides his father's marriage to a distant relative of the earl of Warwick, was to appropriate the legend of Guy of Warwick. Guy was the subject of an Anglo-Norman romance written in the first half of the thirteenth century, telling the story of a great champion who fought against the Viking invasion. The stories are set in the early tenth century, and feature a hero who after pilgrimage to Jerusalem returns incognito and in single combat defeats a Danish giant. He then lives as a hermit in a cave at Guy's Cliffe, north of Warwick, and unrecognized by his wife or neighbours performs acts of charity and piety. There is no good evidence that this Guy ever existed, but William Beauchamp gave the name to his eldest son and ensured that the legend became part of the psychology of the Beauchamps, who handed on down the generations not only the alleged armour of Guy but also the tradition of loyalty and honour.

The only Beauchamp earl to bear the name of their mythical ancestor was born about 1271, and inherited the title on the death of William in 1298. Guy was much more prominent in national affairs than his father had been, and was one of the principal players in the Piers Gaveston affair. Gaveston was the 'favourite', and allegedly the homosexual lover, of Edward II, and had been banished by Edward I who believed that the knight was a bad influence on his son. On his deathbed, Edward I made Guy promise that he would do all he could to prevent Gaveston's return to England, and to keep him away from his son. This was to no avail, for Edward II recalled Gaveston, and gave him the title of earl of Cornwall, along with lands to provide him with a substantial income. Edward, who became king in 1307, gained a reputation for being idle, frivolous and incompetent, and when in 1308 he appointed Gaveston as regent while he went abroad, the nobles were incensed. Gaveston, who called Guy Beauchamp the 'black dog of Arden' was kidnapped by Beauchamp and a group of nobles in June 1312 and taken to Warwick Castle. A few days later he was taken to Blacklow Hill, two miles north of Warwick, and beheaded. It is significant that Blacklow was on the duke of Lancaster's land, belonging to Kenilworth Castle. Lancaster's wealth and independence made him virtually untouchable by the king. Edward continued his capricious reign until Parliament forced his abdication in January 1327, and he was murdered at Berkeley Castle, a place which was to have strong Beauchamp connections, later the same year.

Of Guy's personal life, little is known. He married Alice, his second wife, in 1402, and she bore him six children in their first five years of marriage. Other children were born later, and they may have produced as many as nine in total. He was clearly well educated, being described a 'bene literatus', which probably meant at least that he was competent at Latin, and perhaps that he had spent some time at University. Unusually for nobles at the time, he possessed an excellent library, which has been described as 'one of the most interesting book collections of the fourteenth century'.[5] A selection of forty-two books, which represented only part of his library was given in 1306 to Bordesley Abbey where he was to be buried. Works on surgery, philology, lives of the saints, historical stories and 'romances' were included. A chronicler of Edward II wrote that 'in wisdom and council Guy held no peer'.[6] When Guy died in 1315 there were rumours that he had been poisoned on the orders of Edward II in revenge for his part in the death of Piers Gaveston. The Beauchamp dynasty now suffered a potential hiccough, for Guy's eldest surviving son, Thomas, was not yet two years old.

The danger which lay in an earl dying before his son had reached the age of majority was that his estates were liable to be held by the Crown, and administered by appointed agents. With no adult male to oversee the family affairs, exploitation and neglect were common. Despite a promise to Guy that his executors could administer the estates, within two years Edward II had appropriated the Beauchamp estates and handed them over to agents; no doubt considerable losses were suffered during the early 1320s. Around 1330, the union having been contracted at a very young age, Thomas married Katherine, the daughter of Roger Mortimer who, although she brought no great fortune to the marriage, did bring a good name and influence. They were to produce nine daughters and five sons.

Thomas was a lifelong friend and confidante of the new monarch Edward III, who was to make a huge impact not only on the fourteenth, but also on the following century. There is some evidence which suggests that Thomas may have spent much of his early years growing up in the royal household where he would have formed a close relationship with Edward, who was two years his senior. By 1332 Thomas was governor of the Channel Isles, and his subsequent rise through the military hierarchy was meteoric. He was captain of the army in Edward's campaign against Scotland in 1337, and from 1339 until his death in 1369 he was involved in all the initial engagements of the Hundred Years War. He commanded the fleet transporting the army to Flanders in 1345, and in the following year was, together with the Black Prince, one of the two commanders at the battle of Crécy, where the longbow made its first real impact on warfare. In 1350 he was made one of the inaugural Knights of the Garter, the new order of chivalry devised by Edward III for his closest and most trusted associates, and was created Marshal of England in 1353. At the battle of Poitiers in 1356 he captured the Archbishop of Sens, for whom he gained the enormous ransom of £8,000. A chronicler reported that Thomas 'fought so long and so stoutly, as that his hand was galled with the exercise of his Sword and Pole Axe'. His reputation as a soldier was unparalleled, except by the Black Prince himself. Walsingham the English historian wrote about one incident when the French were so terrified by reports of the arrival of the earl of Warwick that they fled even before he had time to disembark from his ship. In 1365 he joined the Crusades alongside Teutonic knights, and returned with the infant son of a Saracen prince of Lithuania whom he had baptized in London, naming him Thomas and himself standing as Godfather. As a diplomat Thomas took part in two significant missions, being a negotiator at the treaty of Arras, and also being sent to the Pope to argue the justice of England's claim to the French crown. His grandson Richard was to become the most significant diplomat of the early fifteenth century.

Thomas did not neglect his business and family affairs during his long and distinguished military career. In 1354 he acquired the Lordship of Gower after a long legal dispute with the Mowbray family which had started in his grandfather's time. Gower was to move in and out of Beauchamp possession a number of times, and it was never entirely secure for them. It was a particularly profitable dominion because not only did it produce excellent revenue from wool and trading through the ports, but the coal mining industry was beginning to develop. Thomas added many smaller parcels of land and a range of manors to the Beauchamp portfolio, probably investing most of his profits from the war in this way. There were three principal ways of gaining financially from the war. The simplest, but least lucrative, was pay. Thomas was retained by the king and would have been paid a daily wage while at war, as well as the expenses of his retinue and followers. More money could be made from spoils. The conquering army saw itself as free to take anything from the beaten soldiers or towns. Armour, clothing, stores, and especially jewels and plate were taken, as was anything else of value. However, the most important source of income for a senior commander such as Warwick was ransom. The capture of important prisoners could bring massive reward – Thomas' £8,000 for the Archbishop of Sens was the largest ransom paid in the fourteenth century. By the time of his death Thomas owned land from Castle Barnard in County Durham to manors in Cornwall.

Of Thomas's five sons, only two survived into adulthood. William, the fourth son to be born, was sent to Oxford in 1358 to train for the Church, and is the first English peer definitely known to have received a University education. When two of William's older brothers died, the margin for error in the succession was too fine, and so his father extricated him from his clerical career and he became a soldier. His marriage brought the Lordship of Abergavenny to the Beauchamps, and on the death of William's daughter-in-law in 1435, this estate reverted to the main male line and became Richard's. The Beauchamps were fortunate in that additions to the family pool of land gained by younger sons in time generally added to the wealth of the head of the house.

Thomas died in Calais in 1369 of the plague. He willed to be buried in Warwick, the first of the Beauchamp earls not to go back to Worcestershire for interment, and 'that his executors should new build the choir of the Collegiate Church in Warwick where he purposed to be buried.' His fine tomb with its effigy of alabaster and his wife Katherine alongside still survives in excellent condition in the centre of the chancel at St Mary's. Of particular interest are the miniature alabaster figures of mourners or 'weepers' around the sides of the tomb for they give a clear indication of contemporary dress in the late fourteenth century. Thomas' wealth at his death can be seen in his will. He left many gifts of jewellery, silver, gold, rings, crosses and relics. Most significantly, he left to his eldest surviving son, also called Thomas, the sword and coat of mail which had belonged to the legendary Guy. The provenance of this important relic is unknown.

Earl Guy had been outspoken and involved in major political intrigues. Thomas, by contrast, had been totally loyal to the king, had served faithfully and well, and had greatly extended the family wealth and influence. His son, also called Thomas, was to be even more at the centre of disagreement with the crown than had been his grandfather. It is not coincidental that the two setbacks to the Beauchamps' rise in influence and wealth were both in the reigns of monarchs whom historians have generally judged to be either incompetent or deliberately wayward – Edward II and Richard II.

The second Thomas Beauchamp was probably born in early 1339. He does not seem to have had the flair and energy of his father, but the *National Dictionary of Biography*'s description of a person 'retiring and somewhat indolent in disposition' is an unfair exaggeration, for at times he showed flashes both of good sense and of courage. Thomas became earl at the age of thirty, and was certainly in his father's shadow. The English victories in the opening phase of the Hundred Years' War had reached a temporary pause with the treaty of 1360 and the French successes in the early 1370s. Thomas did take part in some incidents in France, accompanying John of Gaunt in the expedition of 1373, but Edward III's encroaching senility and Richard II's lack of interest in the campaign meant that opportunities for distinguished service, and therefore for rewards and spoils, were fewer. Thomas's main impact was on domestic politics in the 1380s and 1390s. Richard II had become king in 1377 at the age of ten, and found himself monarch of a country ravaged by plague and oppressed by taxes to pay for the war across the Channel. That Richard was developing a reputation for an extravagant lifestyle, lavishly rewarding his favourites, and for an ungovernable temper, only added to the increasing tension in government. In 1379 parliament insisted that the king should have a 'governor' to curb his tendencies to excess, and Thomas Beauchamp was appointed.

Dissent was developing on two seemingly unconnected fronts. John Wycliffe and his followers were questioning Papal authority and the philosophy which underlay the doctrine of transubstantiation in the eucharist, and were arguing for the Bible to be available in English. Tradesmen, merchants and land-workers were complaining about the level of taxation, and were struggling under labour shortages and the economic collapse following the plague. The link between the two movements was the questioning of traditional authority, a questioning which was to gather pace for the next century and to bring the medieval order of society to its end. The imposition of the Poll Tax in 1380 ignited the smouldering discontent. Parliament demanded a payment of three groats per annum from everyone over the age of fifteen. Duke and labourer were to pay the same amount, but for a duke a shilling was negligible, while for a peasant it was a month's wages. A movement which seemed to be spontaneous began in the South-east, centred on Kent and Essex, and crowds marched to London in June 1381, with Wat Tyler of Kent, a veteran of the French expeditions, acting as spokesman. The term 'Peasants Revolt' is a misnomer – artisans and tradesmen were as much involved as peasants, suggesting that the issues were wider than the payment of a shilling. This is confirmed by the presence of large numbers of returned soldiers who were complaining that the promises to them of good pay on their return to England had not been met. Having taken Maidstone and Rochester castles, the rebels rampaged in London, burning and pillaging much of the city, including John of Gaunt's Savoy Palace which was blown up with its own supply of gunpowder. The king was barricaded in the Tower of London with Warwick and Henry Bolingbroke, Gaunt's son. Richard II, approaching fifteen, rode with Thomas Beauchamp to Mile End to meet the rebels, and agreed to their demands. A few days later at another meeting, at which the king and Warwick were also present, Tyler was fatally wounded by the mayor of London and the rebellion dispersed. The young king, supported by Thomas, had acted bravely and with a degree of statesmanship. But the warning that he and Parliament should moderate their demands on the common people was not heeded, and the concessions made by Richard

II and Thomas in their negotiations with the rebels were ignored. The chronicler Froissart, observing from France, wrote about the early 1380s that, 'There fell in England great mischief and rebellion of moving of the common people, by which deed England was at a point to have been lost without recovery.'

Some seven months after the rebellion, Thomas's wife Margaret gave birth to their first child. Their son was born on 28 January 1382 at Salwarpe, near Droitwich in Worcestershire, a favourite manor of the Beauchamps from the time before they inherited the Warwick title. He was named Richard after his two godfathers, King Richard and Richard Scrope, Bishop of Lichfield, who was later to become Archbishop of York. His godmother was his aunt Joan, Lady Abergavenny.

Trouble was clearly developing again by 1384 when in the Parliament meeting at Salisbury, at which Thomas was present, the earl of Arundel made an angry speech blaming the extravagant court and the bad advice of the king's friends for the parlous state of the nation. Richard's reply illustrates his growing reputation for ill temper, and did little to ease the situation: 'If you charge me with the responsibility for bad governance, you lie in your throat. Go to the devil.' Rumours of conspiracies were rife, and it seems that only the presence of John of Gaunt, Richard's uncle and the eldest surviving son of Edward III, was holding the situation together. As soon as Gaunt went abroad in 1387, Gloucester (the seventh and youngest son of Edward III), Warwick and Arundel met with their private armies at Waltham Cross and made an 'appeal of treason', accusing the king's friends and advisors of leading him into dangerous errors of lifestyle and policy. In Parliament on 17 November the three 'Lords Appellant' put their case, and took the precaution of wearing chainmail and taking bodyguards with them. They clearly expected that their reception would be less than friendly. By now the earl of Nottingham and Henry Bolingbroke had joined them. It seems that Gloucester

---

I

This Pageant sheweth the birth of the famous knyght Richard Beauchamp Earl of Warrewik which was born in the Maner of Salwarpe in the Counte of Worcester the xxviij day of the Moneth of Januar'. the yere of the Incarnacion of our lorde Jhesu Criste mcclxxxj whose notable actes of chevalry and knyghtly demenaunce been also shewed in the pagentis hereafter ensuying.

This plate showing Richard's birth is typical of the form of the Pageants. The architecture is stylized and there is rarely any suggestion that the places shown are accurately depicted. There is interesting detail in the minor characters in the picture: the woman on the left is stirring food with a spoon, while the woman at the foot of the bed is examining cups in a chest, probably meant to represent gifts to the new-born baby. Richard's mother, Margaret Ferrers, seems to be wearing no bedclothes. The date given is 28 January 1381, although the actual year of Richard's birth was 1382.

his figure sheweth the birth of the famous knyght Richard Beauchamp Erle of
Warwick, which was born in the maner of Salwarp in the Counte of Worcestr the
xxviij day of the apostell of Ianuar. the yere of the Incarnacion of our lord Ih-
esu Crist M.CCC.lxxxij. Whoos notable acttes of Chevalrie and knyghtly demerit-
ees also shewed in the paientes hereafter ensuyng.

I

II

II

Here is shewed howe he was baptised having to his godfadres Kyng Richard the secun and seynt Richard Scrope then bisshop of lichefield and after in process of tyme he was Archebisshope of Yorke.

We do not have the date of Richard's baptism, but it is likely to have followed normal practice at the time and been held within a week of his birth. This makes it unlikely that the king and the bishop would have been present in person; they were probably godparents by proxy. The name Richard was undoubtedly given in honour of the child's godfathers as it was not a name previously used in the family. Richard Scrope was involved in the Percy rebellion as Archbishop of York and Beauchamp was instrumental in his execution for treason.

---

and Arundel were in favour of deposing the king immediately. Thomas counselled more moderate action and besides, the king's closest associate, de Vere, the earl of Oxford, was marching to London with his army. The protesting Lords defeated de Vere at Eynsham on the Thames and Richard II, who again was taking refuge in the Tower, was forced to agree to a long list of demands. A committee of five, including Beauchamp, was appointed to administer the government, and the king was compelled to submit all his expenditure and personal affairs to them. The 'Merciless Parliament' which followed ordered the death or exile of all Richard II's close friends, and he became a mere cipher, with no power. The Lords Appellant were now the government, and were awarded £20,000 by Parliament for their 'great expenses in saving the kingdom and bringing traitors to justice.' Since one of their major complaints had been the extravagance of the court, this payment is not without irony.

Before long Richard II struck back. In May 1389 Gaunt was on his way home from Spain. The king went to Parliament and called the Appellants' bluff, announcing that he would now take over the reigns of government himself. There are indications that he had learned something, for he kept the Lords Appellant on his council, and the next seven years were relatively quiet. Thomas Beauchamp retired from political life to Warwick and the early 1390s saw him complete two major building projects. By 1391 the Chancel of St Mary's was completed around his parents' tomb. The flying ribs which support the vault of the ceiling are unusual – Bristol Cathedral is the only other example. In 1393 the nave was completed, but this no longer stands, having been burned down in the fire of Warwick which destroyed most of the town centre in 1694. Also built in the early 1390s was the north-east tower of Warwick Castle, now known as Guy's Tower, completed at a cost of £395 5s 2d.

While Thomas occupied himself with domestic matters, the king bided his time. The dispute over the Lordship of Gower which had rumbled on through most of the fourteenth century between the Beauchamps and the Mowbrays (the current head of which family was now the earl of Nottingham) again reached a critical point. The case was taken to Parliament, and Warwick lost. Stubbornly refusing to accept the judgement, he was fined and censured, and Richard II may have interpreted this as a sign of Beauchamp's weakness. Rumours of the king's insanity were growing for he would retreat to his throne room, sitting for a whole day wearing his crown and speaking to no-one. The Appellants, again disturbed by Richard II's growing instability, met in August 1397 and swore to put the king, Lancaster and York in prison. Nottingham informed the monarch of the plot, and he acted quickly. Gloucester was captured and taken to Calais where he died in suspicious circumstances. Arundel was executed. Warwick appeared before Parliament and, wrote an eyewitness, 'like a wretched old woman he made confession of all, wailing and weeping and whining', and claimed that Gloucester had persuaded him to enter the conspiracy against his will. The king was delighted with Beauchamp's grovelling posture: 'Thomas of Warwick, your confession is more pleasing to me than the value of all the lands of the Duke of Gloucester and the earl of Arundel.' Beauchamp's possessions were confiscated, and he was exiled to the Isle of Man where he was harshly treated. After about a year he was moved to the Tower of London, being held in a tower which became known as the Beauchamp Tower. The Beauchamp family fortunes were at their lowest ebb.

However, Thomas was not to remain in prison much longer. Henry Bolingbroke, exiled in France, saw his opportunity while Richard II was campaigning in Ireland, and landed with a large force. The king was captured and abdicated in September 1399, Bolingbroke becoming Henry IV. In February 1400 the deposed king starved to death at Pontefract Castle, whether voluntarily or otherwise is not known. Thomas was restored to his possessions and lands (minus Gower), and went to live out his closing years in Warwick. His will was written at the castle on 1 April 1400, and directed that all his friends attending his funeral should be entertained well, with a supper following the service, and a dinner the following day, and that money should be distributed to the poor. He bequeathed to his son Richard, in addition to his estates and lands, 'a bed of silk embroidered with bears', a collection of tapestries depicting the story of Guy of Warwick, and Guy's armour. Additions had obviously been made to the collection of Guy's relics, for Thomas included the 'ragged staves of Guy' in the gift to his son. The earls of Warwick, in addition to using the bear as their emblem, also sported the 'ragged staff', probably a stylization of the tree trunks which Guy reputedly used as weapons against his enemies. Thomas died on 8 July 1401, followed by Margaret his wife four and a half years later. They were buried in the south transept of St Mary's, Warwick and a canopied table tomb erected with a brass memorial to them both. The tomb was destroyed in the fire of 1694, but the brass survives.

2

Richard's Early Years

It is rare to know anything of the detail of the early life of a person in the middle ages. We do not even know the date of birth of Henry V, and although it was not expected when he was born that he would become king, this does give an indication of the lack of interest in childhood of even the most important families. Inevitably, therefore, we have only a few firm facts relating to Richard Beauchamp's first seventeen years. We can, however, reach some conclusions about the likely course of his upbringing based on the handful of known details and on deductions from comparisons with other contemporary families of similar rank.

An illustrated biography of Richard, produced some years after his death, survives in the British Library. Generally referred to as The Pageants of Richard Beauchamp, it consists of 53 line drawings on 28 leaves of vellum, measuring 11in by 8in. Each page depicts an episode from Richard's life, with a brief English text on each. The Pageants end with two genealogical tables showing Richard's descendants, and these latter both help us to date the document and give some indications as to its likely purpose. Whatever the intention lying behind its production, it has no rivals as a unique work of late medieval biography and illustration.

The Pageants follow Beauchamp from his birth 'in the Maner of Salwarp in the Counte of Worcester', through his chivalrous exploits, battles and participation in national affairs, to his death in 1439 and the transportation of his body from Rouen home to Warwick. It places great emphasis on his victories in jousts, and on his loyal service to three kings, portraying him as an ideal model conforming to the code of chivalrous behaviour. Richard is held up as an example of loyalty, bravery and knighthood. His character is praised by the famous and powerful throughout Europe; he 'ful notably and manly behaved himself' on many occasions, and his value to the House of Lancaster is stressed. The Pageants emphasize Richard's role in ensuring the royal succession, particularly in negotiating the marriage of Henry V to Katharine, the daughter of Charles VI of France, and in caring for their infant son, Henry VI.

For the modern reader, however, there are disappointments, for the work gives no clues to Richard as a character. It leaves us unaware of his temperament, his motivation or his individuality. It does not mention his marriages except in the genealogies, and there is nothing about the important trial and execution of Joan of Arc. So why were the Pageants produced? If the document it is not a biography in the modern sense, what precisely is it? The genealogies at the end of the book might give some clues to its purpose, and perhaps also some indication of its level of reliability. The first of these two genealogies shows Richard, his two wives, and his five children – three daughters by his first wife, Elisabeth, and a son and daughter by his second wife, Isabel. The second genealogy shows his daughter Anne's marriage to Richard Neville (Warwick the Kingmaker). Their daughter, also named Anne, married firstly Prince Edward, son of Henry VI, and then Richard, duke of Gloucester, who became king in 1483. Their son Edward Plantagenet, who died in 1484 is also depicted. This suggests that the Pageant dates from between the mid-1480s and 1493 when Anne died. Writers have generally suggested that it was commissioned by Anne after Richard III's death at Bosworth to draw attention to the plight of her noble family, now in relative poverty and disgrace because the Kingmaker supported the losing side in the Wars of the Roses.[7] The dating is, however, less straightforward than this, for the two genealogies are unfinished. The coats of arms on the first family tree have been started, but only those of Richard and his first wife approach completion; the others are only sketched in outline. In the final page, no attempt has been made to draw the arms, but the blank shields which were to contain them have been drawn. Besides, and most importantly, the style of handwriting on the two genealogies clearly differs from that which is used in the bulk of the Pageants.

Thus, the most plausible explanation is that the genealogies were added some time after the completion of the main document to validate Anne's claim for the restoration of her inheritance which had been confiscated following the deaths of Richard Neville her husband and Richard III her son-in-law. If this is the case, when might the bulk of the Pageants have been produced? The most likely occasion is the transfer of Richard Beauchamp's body from its temporary resting place in the south transept of St Mary's, Warwick, to its permanent home in the completed chantry chapel which had been provided for in his will. This would date the main document fairly precisely to 1475, with the two genealogical pages being added about a decade later.

We must also beware of assuming that the Pageants consistently relate reliable historical detail. At some points it is manifestly mistaken – for example, Richard returns from pilgrimage to the Holy Land to find Henry V on the throne, whereas in reality he came home some three years before Henry succeeded his father. In other places, however, it seems to be remarkably accurate, and the suggestion that the majority of it represents Richard's own memories as told to his children and related to the chronicler by Anne is not unlikely.

In the opening scene of the Pageants, we see Richard's mother in a four-poster bed, apparently without clothing, attended by four ladies, one of whom holds the baby. The second scene shows the importance of the child – his godfathers are the king and the future Archbishop of York. From outside the Pageants there is evidence that the young Richard spent some time in the royal court, as was normal for the sons of the higher nobility, and he is mentioned in this context at least twice. We have no details of his education, but we do know that later in life he was fluent in French and was not only a brilliant tactician in war, but was also a very capable manager of one of the most significant land holdings of the middle ages. His contemporaries such as Henry Bolingbroke, also educated in the royal household, were taught Latin, spelling and grammar, and although Richard was sixteen years Henry's junior, he grew up in the same milieu. Moreover, he certainly came from a family which valued education – his great-grandfather was noted for his learning, his uncle had been to Oxford and the family possessed a library. It was normal for boys such as Richard to learn the skills of jousting and warfare early in life, and Richard's proficiency at these when he was barely out of his teens suggests that his upbringing did not neglect his physical development.

At the age of ten, in September 1392, Richard was contracted to marry Elisabeth, the daughter of Lord Berkeley. Elisabeth was not yet seven, but was the only child of Lord Berkeley. The intention behind the contract was the alliance of two great families, and the prestige and increase in influence which this would bring to both houses. They were married by 5 October 1397, at the ages of fifteen and twelve. Following the exile of Richard's father, Thomas II, the young couple were placed in the custody of the duke of Surrey. Richard and Elisabeth were to produce three children, all daughters, and all of whom were to survive infancy. Their eldest child, Margaret, was born at Goodrest Manor, which belonged to Kenilworth Castle and was situated about two miles north of Warwick, 'the next year after the battle of Shrewsbury' (i.e. 1404). She died in 1467. The second child, Eleanor, was born at Walthamstow, a Beauchamp family manor east of London, 'shortly after the feast of our Lady's nativity' (8 September) in 1408, and the third, Elisabeth, was born at Warwick Castle, but we have no date for her birth.

The effect of the affair of the Lords Appellant on Richard, and of his father's subsequent imprisonment and exile, can only be guessed at. Great uncertainty about the family's future must have been generated and when, shortly after Richard's marriage, the Beauchamp estates were confiscated, the prospects for the dynasty which had steadily increased its wealth and influence throughout the fourteenth century looked decidedly insecure. Later in life, Richard was to be totally loyal to the crown, and seemed to distance himself from political factions and intrigues; perhaps the experience of watching the stresses of 1387, and his father's decline a decade later had impressed upon him the danger of quarrelling with the monarch. On the other hand, when Bolingbroke became king in 1399, to belong to a family which had been prominent in the protest against Richard II's injustices was no bad thing. The Beauchamps were again in favour. The seventeen year old Richard was installed as a Knight of the Bath on the eve of Henry's coronation – an honour which is illustrated in the third panel of the Pageant. At the ceremony the next day, Richard's father, restored from imprisonment and disgrace, carried in procession behind the king a sheathed sword, signifying mercy.

III

Here sheweth how this noble lorde Richard Beauchamp Erle of Warrewik was made Knyghte to the whiche ordre in procession of tyme as shall appere folowyng by his noble actes he did greet hnour & worship.

Richard was made a Knight of the Order of the Bath at the age of seventeen, on the eve of the coronation of Henry IV. Along with his father, now restored to his lands following his fall from favour under Richard II, he took part in the ceremonies the next day. The rich decorations on the robes of the attendants are typical of the level of detail shown on clothing in the Pageants.

The middle ages was a time of great superstition – incidents pointing towards good or ill were taken very seriously – and so when two events happened at the coronation which were taken as bad omens, the future for the reign of Henry IV did not look promising. When the new king was anointed with the holy oil believed to have been blessed by Thomas Beckett, his beard was found to be crawling with lice. Then a little later in the service he dropped a gold 'noble', the coin which he was to give at the offertory. Those who were able to understand such signs predicted a troubled period. Less than two years after the coronation, Richard became the fifth Beauchamp earl of Warwick when Thomas II died on 8 July 1401.

Almost as soon as Henry was crowned, rebellion began to stir, and he was never to be totally free of accusations that he had usurped the crown. Even after Richard II's death there were rumours that he was still alive and in Scotland, but the main problem which was to drag on for the whole of the first decade of the fifteenth century was the Welsh rebellion led by Owain Glyndwr. Often portrayed in legend as a wild and uncultured barbarian from the hills, Glyndwr was in fact a gentleman landowner. He had studied law in London, had fought under Richard II against the Scots, and had been with Arundel's forces in the defeat of de Vere during the Appellants' protests. The trouble seemed to begin when Glyndwr and his neighbour, Lord Grey of Ruthyn, fell out over a disputed piece of land, and then Grey failed to deliver a summons to Glyndwr for his support of Henry on the Scottish borders. His non-attendance was interpreted as treason, and so when Glyndwr appeared before Parliament to put his case against Grey over the land dispute, the king was not well disposed. He dismissed Glyndwr offensively : 'What care we for these barefoot Welsh doggis?'

Glyndwr's anger ignited a smouldering resentment against English domination along the Welsh borders, and a series of raids made by his followers made rapid gains. The area seemed out of control, and the Welsh were able to raid and attack at will. Henry planned a three-pronged attack in September 1402. His son and heir, Prince Henry, aged only sixteen but under the guidance of Henry Percy, better known as Hotspur, would lead the attack against North Wales, with the king attacking the centre and Richard Beauchamp leading his forces from Hereford into South Wales. Richard's presence in the Welsh

III

campaigns was more than simply service to the king – Beauchamp estates in Worcestershire and along the borders with Wales were at risk, and he had not forgotten that the Lordship of Gower in South Wales, lost by Thomas II, might one day be returned to the family. The English forces crossed the border to be greeted by three weeks of continuous heavy rain. The rivers were swollen and mostly uncrossable, and one of the main problems for any medieval army was finding accessible river crossings. By the end of September the English retreated without having made any serious contact with the Welsh. Glyndwr was already gaining a reputation for sorcery, and the English soldiers now became convinced that he was able to call up storms to defeat them. Bad weather seemed to run all through Henry IV's reign – a sign that the omens at his coronation had been interpreted correctly.

On 26 February 1403 King Henry's new bride, Joan of Navarre was crowned Queen at Westminster Abbey. As was customary, the celebrations were accompanied by a jousting tournament and Richard Beauchamp, less than a month after his twenty-first birthday, was the Queen's champion, defending her honour 'ageynst alle other comers'. The illustration in the Pageants shows Richard in full armour, with his helmet surmounted with his crest of the bear and ragged staff, and the king and Queen watching the event from a box. The level of detail in the Pageants is apparent from this scene. In the foreground two spectators climb a tree for a better view, and others squabble over a broken lance, no doubt a valuable souvenir. Richard was obviously coming closer to the centre of power.

As befitted someone with such close connection to the Crown, Richard was also developing his literary taste. He owned a large volume produced at the beginning of the fifteenth century which was 'an informative and instructive collection of reading material with a debate on the nature of spiritual and temporal power, a staunch defence of the established Church by way of an attack on the friars, and a popular and comprehensive history.'[8] Now in the British Library, and known as the 'Trevisa Manuscript' because of its association with John Trevisa, chaplain to Lord Berkeley, this

---

IV

Here shewes how this noble lorde Dan Jone Duches of Breteyn doughter of the Kyng of Navern and newe wedded wif to henry the iiijth of Englond was Crowned Quene of this noble Reame of Englond.

Joan of Navarre's coronation took place in Westminster Abbey on 26 February 1403, following her marriage to Henry three weeks earlier at Winchester Cathedral. This is one of the few pictures in which Richard Beauchamp does not feature directly. Whether he is meant to be one of the attendants depicted on the left is not indicated. The importance of this scene is that it sets the stage for the Lancastrian succession – the dynasty to the service of which Richard was to devote his diplomatic and military career.

Here shewes howe dan Iane Duches of Breteyn doughter of the kyng of
Nabern. and nowe wedded wif to Henry the iiijth kyng of England was
Crowned Quene of this noble Reaume of England

IV

27

Here shewes howe atte Coronacion of Quene Jane, Erle Richard
kepte Justice for the Quenes pars ageynst all other commers Where
he so notably and so knyghtly behaved hym self, as redounded
to his noble fame and ppetuell worship.

V

V

Here shewes howe atte Coronacion of Quene Jane Erle Richard Kepte Justes for the Quenes part ageynst all other comers Where he so notably and so knyghtly behaved hym self as redounded to his noble fame and perpetuall worship.

Jousting is a major theme in the Pageants and serves to emphasize Richard's place in the tradition of chivalry. This plate shows the lively and detailed observation which the artist brings to the illustrations. The king and queen are at the top of the picture, watching from a balcony. The master of the joust is on the left, inspecting spears held up to him by an attendant. The right-hand panel shows a jouster preparing for combat, while in the right foreground two onlookers squabble over a broken lance, presumably wishing to take it away as a souvenir. Richard is shown in the centre of the picture, identified by the bear and ragged staff on his helmet. This is anachronistic, as the two elements were not combined until about 1450.

---

is clearly for reading rather than display. It is written in a neat hand, with a few modest initials and decoration in the borders. Richard's coat of arms appears on two of the pages as a sign of ownership.

In the spring of 1403 another important omen appeared. A comet, visible throughout Europe, was a source of great speculation about what it portended. In England it was thought to signify 'greet deth and blodeshede', and was linked to the general unrest of the reign and to Glyndwr in particular. The comet is shown in the Pageants above a skirmish between Glyndwr and English forces led by Beauchamp, the text claiming that Richard came close to capturing the rebel, and took his banner. This incident, if it happened at all, is more likely to have been in 1404 near Abergavenny, rather than in 1403 as the Pageant's link with the comet implies.

VI

Here shewes howe at thies daies appered a blasyng sterre called stella comata which after the seiyng of Clerkys signyfied greet deth and blodeshede And sone uppon beganne the Warre of Wales by oon Owen of Glendour their chief capteyn. Who, emonges other Erle Richard so sore sewed that he hadde nerehande taken hym and put hym to flight and toke his baner and moche of his people and his banner.

This battle scene is full of action and is dominated by the comet in the top right-hand corner, the appearance of which in the spring of 1403 is well-documented as having been visible throughout Europe. Richard is again identifiable as the central figure by his helmet. The claim in the text that he captured Owen Glyndwr's banner is not confirmed in any other source.

Here shewes howe at thies daues appeered a blasyng sterre called stella comata
which after the seyng of clerkys sygnyfied gret deth and blodshede And sone
vppon beganne the Warre of Wales by oon Owen of Glendour thow chief
capteyn whom emongst other Erle Richard, so sore serued that he hadd
nershande taken hym and put hym to flight and toke hys banere
and moche of hys people and hys banere

VI

Here shewe howe at the batell of Shrowesbury, betwen kyng Henry the
iiijth & S. Henry Percy / Erle Richard there beyng on the kynge parte, ful
notably & manly behaved hym self, to his greet lawde & worship / In
which batell was slayne the said S. Henry Percy and many other w.
hym. And on the kynge party, there was slayne in the kyng cotearm.
chef of other, the Erle of Safford, Erle Richardes Annte son w.
many other in greet nombre, on whoes sowles god haue mcy Amen.

VII

31

VII

The battle of Shrewsbury took place on 21 July 1403. The forces of the king are on the left of the picture, with Beauchamp in the centre. Immediately opposite him is Henry Percy, known as Hotspur, falling backwardss after having been pierced through the breast by an arrow, although a contemporary source describes him as having been shot in the face. In the foreground a footsoldier with a spear stands over a fallen archer.

A Pageants incident which can be dated precisely, and which is clearly accurate, is the battle of Shrewsbury, which took place on 21 July 1403. Discontent with Henry IV was increasing, and the Percy family of Northumberland was in the forefront of unease. The Percys asserted that Henry's original claim had simply been to his inheritance of the Duchy of Lancaster, passed on from his father John of Gaunt, and that he had promised not to seek the crown for himself. Henry Percy, 'Hotspur', had made a tentative alliance with Glyndwr but King Henry, learning of the plot, met Percy's forces at Shrewsbury. This battle was highly significant, not only because it was the first time that two English armies had faced each other with longbows, but also because it settled the question of the royal succession for the next sixty years. The Lancastrian line became much more secure after the defeat of the leading rebels.

VIII

The illustration here shows Richard being invested as a Knight of the Garter, an honour also bestowed on his father and grandfather. The scene is the battlefield at Shrewsbury, with the fortifications of the town in the background on the left. We know that this ceremony took place the day after the battle, though whether the artist was correct in portraying it taking place on the field of battle is less certain. Interestingly, the traditional dubbing with a sword is not shown – instead Richard grasps the King's garter.

In this pagent is shewed howe the noble Erle Richard was made knyght of the Garter at that tyme to his greet worship. And after by marciall act by hym ful notably and knyghtly achieved in his owre persone. Did greet honour & worship to the noble ordre of knyghtes of the Garter. As by the pagent hereafter folowyng more pleynly is shewed.

VIII

33

Glyndwr's forces failed to turn up in support of Percy, perhaps recognizing that they were much more used to fighting in raids and ambushes than in a set-piece battle. When Hotspur was shot through the head as he lifted his visor to gasp for air the Percy revolt collapsed. Prince Henry was wounded by an arrow, which left the right side of his face disfigured. The standard portraits of him from later life show only his left profile. The evening of the battle was marked by another omen as a full eclipse of the moon shed an eerie light over the wounded and dead.

The Pageants depict the Battle of Shrewsbury with Richard in the centre of the action, and in plate VIII Richard receives the Order of the Garter for his bravery from King Henry on the battlefield. The records of the Order show that Beauchamp became a Knight of the Garter on 22 July 1403, the day after the battle, although whether the investiture actually took place on the field as the Pageants suggest is not recorded.

Richard was taking an increasingly prominent part not only on the battlefield, but also at court, and his dual career as soldier and diplomat was beginning to take shape. In October 1403 he was appointed as Captain of Brecon Castle, a key border fortification. A letter written by Richard's secretary John Shirley survives, in which Richard informs the king that many of his retainers were reluctant to go to Wales on a permanent posting, fearing that their interests at home might suffer while they were away. In the king's Council, Mowbray, whose family had for generations been in tension with the Beauchamps, claimed that he should have precedence over Richard. The king decided in Beauchamp's favour, perhaps remembering that Richard's father had opposed Richard II whereas Mowbray had informed on the Appellants.

Glyndwr made the mistake of not attacking the English forces immediately after the battle of Shrewsbury when they were tired and weakened, but the Welsh continued to make ground. In the summer of 1403 Camarthen fell to the Welsh after a short siege, and in 1404 they gained the major strongholds of Cardigan and Aberystwyth. Moreover, the Welsh did not play by the traditional rules of medieval warfare. They captured Conwy Castle on Good Friday, attacking while the garrison were all in chapel. After capturing Harlech, with only three castles remaining in English hands, Glyndwr had himself crowned Prince of Wales. By now the legitimate Prince of Wales, Henry, had been appointed the king's lieutenant in Wales, aged seventeen, and was beginning to show the remarkable organizational skills which were later to be put to use in France. He first argued to the Council that he needed continuity of financing and supply to provision his troops and to relieve the strongholds, and then set about a more regular system of reviewing the army. The effects were not immediate, for in 1404 Glyndwr invaded Herefordshire and reached as far as eight miles east of Worcester. This was uncomfortably close to Beauchamp heartland, and Richard took a leading part in the defence of the borders. From this point Richard and Prince Henry worked increasingly closely together, refining campaign and siege methods against the Welsh which would give them the advantage in France a decade later. Apart from a break in 1408-1409 when Richard went on pilgrimage, he and Henry were to spend almost all of the next eighteen years together, much of the time living in camps. The two young men felt most at home in the company of soldiers, and only made rare excursions into domestic life. During this period, Prince Henry gathered around himself a group of men, with Beauchamp at the centre of them, who were to be with him for the rest of his life, and whose continuing loyalty he was ready to reward.

Despite the decisive result at Shrewsbury, rumblings against Henry IV were not over. Another plot, this time led by Archbishop Scrope of York, took the king and Richard Beauchamp north in 1405. Scrope had manifestos against Henry posted on the doors of churches in York, and had masterminded a plan to divide England into three, between Percy, Mortimer and Glyndwr. Scrope was arrested, along with his fellow conspirator Mowbray, and Beauchamp sat as one of the judges in the trial. He condemned his godfather Scrope and his rival Mowbray to execution, and was given the Lordship of Gower as a reward for his loyalty to the crown. This valuable lordship was now back in Beauchamp hands after being 'on loan' to the Mowbrays for eight years. Richard seems not to have been troubled by the beheading of his godfather, clearly seeing loyalty to the crown as his primary duty.

However, if Richard was untroubled, the king's conscience was not so easy. Already unsettled over accusations that he had no right to the throne, Henry seems to have been smitten with guilt over the execution of Scrope, an act which critics were likening to Henry II's murder of Thomas Beckett. About a week after Scrope's death, the king was incapacitated by a mysterious illness which was interpreted as divine judgement. The nature of his illness has puzzled historians for generations. The main symptom seems to have been a disfiguring skin complaint. An eye-witness described great pustules on his hands and face and wrote that he was 'a lepir and evyr fowlere and fowlere'. A simple diagnosis of leprosy is not, however, adequate. As early as 1390 Henry had paid a barber for blood-letting to relieve him of 'pokkes' and his illness seems to have had intermittent acute episodes which prevented him from functioning, rather than the gradual decline associated with true leprosy. Perhaps the most convincing explanation is that he suffered from a skin disease such as psoriasis which was exacerbated by his extreme feelings of guilt, and that he was incapacitated by episodes of mental collapse.

This illness, whatever its nature, is important for the history of the last seven years of Henry IV's reign. The war against the Welsh rebels, increasing tension with France, and the worsening economy of the country all conspired to make Henry more tortured and less effective. The campaign is Wales was, however, at last turning in favour of the English. Although Glyndwr was reinforced by French troops landing at Milford Haven, Prince Henry, assisted by Beauchamp, began to gain the upper hand. Richard was present at Grosmont in the Monnow valley when a large contingent of Welsh troops was defeated, and the increasing use by the English of heavy artillery began to make an impact. A $4\frac{1}{2}$-ton cannon nicknamed 'the Messenger' was employed, and proved effective in recapturing fortified castles, teaching Henry and Richard the importance of this relatively new technology in siege warfare. At some point in 1405-6 Richard was commanding a fleet of ships in the Bay of Biscay, perhaps trying to prevent French help reaching Wales, and then in 1408 he took a leading part in the siege of Aberystwyth. As Prince Henry took strongholds, he made sure to garrison them securely, learning another important lesson for France. Until 1403 the English had pursued a policy of trying to subdue Wales from the border. Henry recognized that raids conferred no permanent advantage unless the gains were properly defended against reprisals. He developed a practice of putting trusted lieutenants in charge of newly acquired strongholds, while he himself moved with the front line.

Between the first clear Welsh defeats and 1410 the rebellion gradually died out. There was no decisive final encounter, but Prince Henry gradually gained back all the lost ground. Glyndwr went into hiding, and it is not known when or where he died. The years on campaign in Wales had taught the prince and Richard many valuable lessons, which they were further to refine and put to use in France. The supply line, beginning with well-planned finance was essential. Troops had to be fed, armed and paid, and an efficient way of doing this was an important first step in war. Henry also guarded against the medieval practice of commanders claiming wages for soldiers who did not exist, or who had deserted or died, through a thorough system of review. Transport by water was necessary, especially for the heavier items, and the sieges of the coastal castles such as Harlech and Aberystwyth had confirmed this. Control of river crossings was vital, especially in wet seasons, and the use of specialist siege weapons, including the technological cutting edge of cannons, could be decisive.

As the Welsh war began to take less of their attention Prince Henry and Beauchamp became freer to pursue other interests, and for the first time Richard was able to give some serious attention to his own business affairs. His income from his estates for this first decade of the fifteenth century was about £1,400 per annum. He had other income from his wages in the war, and presumably from spoils. This already put him among the leading landowners in the country, but in the next decade he would more than double his estates' profits. This was at a time when the country's economy was generally depressed. The effects of the Black Death continued to affect land prices and profits, and the price of wool, England's main export earner, fell by some 15% in the early 1400s.

At some time in 1408 Richard and Prince Henry went together on pilgrimage to visit the shrine of the obscure saint John of Bridlington in Yorkshire. This journey clearly made an impression on Beauchamp, for in his will almost thirty years later he left a gold statue to the shrine. John of Bridlington had died in 1379 of the plague, and having lived a holy and revered life was canonized in 1401. Prince Henry regarded him with special favour, and it may be that his and Richard's devotion to the saint was connected with the contemporary fear of the plague, since John was credited with powers to keep individuals free from the disease.

3

Jerusalem, Calais and Agincourt

The closing years of Henry IV's reign were marked by worsening ill health and differences with his eldest son. In the winter of 1408-1409 he was seriously unwell, perhaps even close to death, and made his will naming Henry Prince of Wales as his heir. The prince, having spent much of the last six years containing the rebellion in Wales, now seemed to have Glyndwr under control, even if he had not been decisively crushed. A greater sense of responsibility and autonomy had been encouraged among the landowners in the Marches. They had benefited from the support of the monarchy in securing their properties; they must now repay some of the spoils of war which they had received with an increased commitment, financial as well as military, to the defence of the borders. That the Beauchamp family owned considerable stretches of land in the Marches and in Worcestershire committed Richard to this policy. Perhaps more importantly for policy developments at the end of the first decade of the fifteenth century, the Crown was on the verge of serious financial embarrassment.

There were also stirrings from France. The king and the prince both wanted to hold the French to the Treaty of Brétigny, signed in 1360, in which sovereignty over Aquitaine had been conceded to the English Crown in exchange for relinquishing any English claim to the crown of France. Tension developed between the king and the prince not over the rightness of pursuing this settlement, but over the methods to be used. The prince was clearly a man of action, and had developed a taste for war from his Welsh experiences. He saw the widening split between the dukes of Burgundy and Orléans, together with the increasing mental instability of Charles VI, as window of opportunity to cross the channel. His father preferred to wait and to talk. Moreover, with the struggles on the Welsh border virtually ended as Glyndwr seemed to disappear, Prince Henry lacked gainful employment, and was developing a reputation as a wild playboy.

The triple problems of the king's failing health, financial difficulties and the potential for a rift between the king and the Prince of Wales over the question of France meant that the centre of government was under extreme strain. Where was the earl of Warwick during this period of uncertainty? He went abroad for two years. Fourteen of the fifty-five panels of The Pageants of Richard Beauchamp, more than a quarter of the total document, are devoted to Richard's journey to the Holy Land in 1408, and his leisurely return through Europe lasting until some time in late 1409. He was certainly back in England for appointment to the Prince of Wales' Council in January 1410, although the Pageant is mistaken here in its chronology. In Plate XXIII he is shown as arriving home to find Henry V already on the throne; an event which did not happen until 1413. Indeed, at Henry's coronation on 9 April of that year Richard was to act as Steward of England – the chief organizer of the ceremony. As mentioned before, the question of the historical reliability of the Pageant must, therefore, be treated with caution, if not with scepticism.

Plate IX shows Richard's ship being loaded with cloth (presumably for exchange purposes and gifts) and other possessions, followed by his arrival on the other side of the channel in Plate X. Richard then travels to Paris, spending some time with Charles VI, with a Plate showing the king and the earl together at dinner on Whitsunday. The author of the Pageants stresses Richard's courtly bearing: 'He so mannerly behaved hym self in langage & norture that the Kyng and his lordes with all other people gave hym greet lawde.' This visit may be the first hint that Richard's journey was about more than tourism and sightseeing. His closeness to the Prince of Wales, who was becoming increasingly interested in the affairs of government and in particular in the situation in France, makes it more than likely that the talk at dinner was not merely social. Had Richard been sent on an embassy by Prince Henry, whose expectation must have been that in view of his father's illness he would become king very shortly?

Leaving Paris, Richard pays homage to the Pope in Rome (this plate has been comically defaced, probably by a seventeenth-century puritan, to give the Pope

---

IX

Here shewes howe good provision made of English clothe and other thynges necessary and licence hadde of the kyng Erle Richard sailed towards the holy' londe and specially to the holy Cite of Jherusalem Where our lorde Jhesu Criste wilfully suffered his bitter passion for the redemption of al man kynde.

Five years are missing between this and the last illustration. This is the first in a series of fourteen, a quarter of the total Pageants, depicting Richard's pilgrimage to the Holy Land, beginning in 1408. Richard is in the foreground being helped into a small boat, dressed as a pilgrim and carrying a staff. Cloth is being carried by his men on the left, probably to be used as barter on the travels. In the upper part of the picture a ship bearing Richard's insignia waits, with a suggestion of the English Channel cliffs on the left.

Here sheweth howe good provision made of English clothe and other thynge necessary and licence hadde of the kyng. Erle Richard sailed towardes the holy lond and specially to the holy Citte of Iherlm Where oure lord Ihu Criste wilfully suffered his bitter passion for the redempcion of al mankynde.

IX

Here shewes howe Erle Richard; when he was passed the see, he
turned to his noble & mre Cossyn the Due of Barr of whom he mrci
ful louyngly and worshipfully resceibed, and there taried by dius
in greet pleasir

X

X

Here shewes howe Erle Richard, when he was passed the see, he turned to his nole and nere Cosyn the Duc of Barr of whom he was ful lovyngly and worshipfully received and there taried viij daies in greet pleasir.

Having crossed the Channel, Richard mounts a flight of steps on the quayside and is greeted by the Duke of Barr who raises his hat in greeting.

---

and Cardinals silly hats). Next, Richard is shown in a joust, seriously wounding Sir Pandolf Malatete at Verona. This is one of six jousting scenes in the Pageants, which also includes seven battle scenes – six on land and one at sea. The document is keen to portray Richard as a chivalrous knight, in Plate XXV describing Sigismund the Emperor as saying to Henry V, 'no prince cristyn... hadde suche a nother knyght as he hadde of therle of warrewyk, addyng thereto that if al curtesye were lost, yet myght hit be founde ageyn in hym. And so ever after by the Emperor's auctorite, was called the fadre of Curteisy.' The main interest of the author of the Pageants seems to be establishing Richard's credentials within the traditions of European chivalry, to which his involvement in the affairs of state seem almost incidental.

At Venice, Richard is regally received, and is lent a galley and crew to continue his journey. Having spent about six weeks at sea, he arrives in Jerusalem and is shown kneeling at Jesus's sepulchre, where his coat of arms is set next to the tomb as a sign of his piety. A series of three plates then deals with meetings and meals with Sir Baltirdam, 'the Sultan's lieutenant', who rather implausibly tells Richard that the exploits of Guy of Warwick were well known in the area, and that his 'lif they hadde there in bokes of their langage.' It is known that Prince Henry was keen to go on Crusade; was Warwick assessing the situation for his friend? Richard then returns to England via Venice, Russia, Latvia, Prussia, Westphalia and other regions of Germany, taking as long as a year.

This tour may well have fulfilled a number of purposes. Perhaps Richard preferred to be out of England while tension at court ran high. His memories of

---

XI

And here is shewed howe that at this noble Duke's desire Erle Richard his Cosyn rode with him ageyn the Whitsontide to the Cite of Parys the Kyng of Fraunce there then being present in greet Roialte.

The Earl and the Duke are shown approaching the city gates of Paris, followed by their retainers in civilian dress. The gatekeeper leans on a spiked club.

And here is shewed howe that at this noble Duke desire Erle Richard
his Cosyn rode w* hym ageyn the Whisshentide to the Citee of Purys the kyng
of ffraunce there then beyng psent in grett Rialtee.

XI

XII

XII

Here shewes howe on the Whitsonday the Kyng of Fraunce in reverence of the holy feest was Crowned and made Erle Richard to sitte at his table. Where he so manerly behaved hym self in langage ck torture that the Kyng and his lordes with all other people gave hym greet lawde and at his departing the Kyng assigned hym an heraud to geve his attendaunce and conducte hym saufly thorowe all his Reame.

Richard's bearing and courtly status are again emphasised, suggesting that he is a welcome guest in any court. It is unlikely, however, that this is a purely social occasion. Although there had been a pause in hostilities between England and France, the 'Hundred Years War' over the monarchy was still unresolved, and Richard may have been involved in diplomatic talks. The attention to architectural detail in this picture is impressive, and gives the impression of a richly decorated palace.

---

his father's difficulties over the conflicts around the Crown in Richard II's time may have been painful, and he must have been reluctant to put himself in a similar situation undermining the authority of a declining king. He probably also had a genuine desire to see the world, to visit the Holy Land – for there is real evidence of his genuine Christian commitment – and to relax a little after the battles in Wales. Further, it is not stretching probability too far to suggest that he was engaged in talks and reconnaissance for Prince Henry in preparation for his kingship and planned continental expeditions.

In London, the tensions had not eased during Beauchamp's absence. A council was appointed in January 1410 under the leadership of Prince Henry to be

---

XIII

Here shewes howe at his departyng porn Fraunce into Lumbardy the frenche herawde richely rewarded and licenced. In shorte space after come a nother herowde to Erle Richard sent from Sir Pandolf Malatete or Malet with lettres of chalenge to do certeyn poyntes of hermes with hym at Verona at a certeyn day assigned for the ordre of the Garter To the which chalenge to be doon before Sir Galeot of Mantua. Erle Richard gladly agreed and after he hadde doon his pilgremage at Rome he retorned to Verona where he and his chalenger Sir Pandolf shulde first Just then go to gedres with axes after with armyng swerde and last with sharpe daggers.

Two scenes are depicted in this plate. In the main part, Richard is mounted front-facing, saying goodbye to the French herald on his right, and receiving the challenge from the second herald on his left. In the smaller scene, Richard is presented to the Pope. The Pope's tiara has been defaced, and the Cardinal standing next to him has had ridiculous feathers added to his hat, probably by a seventeenth-century Puritan.

Here sheweth howe at his departyng from ffraunce into Lumbardy, the frenche heroldes richely rewarded and licenced. In shorte space after come a nother heroldes to Erle Richard, sent from from ye Pandolf ayalette or ayalet wt lres of chalenge, to do certeyn poyntes of armes wt hym at Veron at a certeyn day assigned for the ordre of the Garter, so the which chaleng to be doon before ye Talbot of ayantua. Erle Richard gladly agreed. And after he hadde doon his pilgremage at Rome, he retorned to Veron, where he & his chalenger ye Pandolf shuld ffirst just, then go togedre wt axes after wt armyng swerdes and last wt sharpe daggers

XIII

XIV

XIV

Howe atte place and day assigned, resortyng thidre all the Contre, Sir Pandolf entered the place ix speres born before hym. Then thacte of speres to therle Richard worshipfully finisshed after went they to gedre with axes and if the lorde Galaot hadde nat the sonner cried peas Sir Pandolfe sore wounded on the lifte shuldre hadde been utterly slayne in the felde.

This plate, and its commentary continue the theme of Richard's chivalrous exploits, building his reputation as the most skilled knight in Europe. In the centre of the balcony, Sir Galaot holds a baton, which he would throw down to end the fight when it became clear that one of the combatants was likely to die.

---

responsible for day-to-day government during the king's illness. It was composed mainly of associates of Prince Henry who had fought with him in the campaigns against Wales, and Richard was naturally a member. This pattern was to continue. Prince Henry had spent his formative years on the battlefield in the company of aristocratic soldiers. He felt at ease with them, and trusted their judgement. The men who were beside him in Wales now came into increasing prominence as he moved closer to his inheritance, and were to constitute the core of his inner circle for the rest of his life.

Finance continued to be a problem, and constituted the major business at most of the fourteen meetings of the council between January 1410 and its dissolution in 1411. France was, however, attracting more of the Prince of Wales' attention. At the opening of Parliament in 1410 Henry Beaufort, bishop of Winchester and half-brother of Henry IV, described the duke of Burgundy as a major threat to the security of Calais, England's long-established foothold on the continent. The tension between the factions in France, focused on the two houses of Burgundy and Orléans, had not been helped by Burgundy plotting the murder of Orléans

---

XV

How Erle Richard came to Venise and was Inned at Seynt Georges and was right worshipfully received of the Duc and lordes of Venise and many Roial presentes hadde he there given hym And moche the rather for the greet lawde they herde was geven hym at Verona.

The treatment of Venice in this picture is conventional, and there is little to suggest that the artist knew of its unique position. The Duc, at the bottom right, greets Richard, and wears an elaborately decorated baldrick, but there is no hint of the distinctive ducal cap worn by the Doges. The page holding Richard's horse has the ragged staff clearly marked on his chest.

How Erle Richard come to Venise and was lined at Seynt George, and was right worshipfully resceived of the Duc e lordes of Venise, and many fyne presentis hadd he there yeven hym, And moche the rather for the grete laude they herde was yeven hym at Veron

XV

Here shewes howe Erle Richard Nue Worthely resceded by the Patriarke Deputie at Jerm, and licensed to comune in deu forume with the hethen people and specially with the greet astate if the caus required, and howe to them he shulde be demeaned

XVI

XVI

Here shewes howe Erle Richard was worthely received by the Patriarkes depute at Jerusalem and licenced to commune in deu fourme with the hethen people and specially with the greet astates is the caus required and howe with them he shulde be demeaned.

The Patriarch's deputy, carrying the double cross, greets Richard as he disembarks in the Holy Land. The hills topped by trees in the background give an impression of the artist's idea of what the Holy Land looked like. Why he should be given special permission to meet 'hethen people' is unclear – is he engaged in cultural tourism, or is he undertaking some diplomatic mission.

---

on the streets of Paris in 1407. Sending embassies to London in 1411, Burgundy asked for help from England in his struggles, perhaps promising to enforce the 1360 Treaty in return. Prince Henry seems to have been enthusiastic about the suggestion, whereas the king was non-committal.

In September 1410 Warwick travelled with Prince Henry to France, apparently for only a short time. They may have been in contact with the duke of Burgundy, laying the foundations for Henry's planned action. On 2 October 1410 Prince Henry retained Richard 'for life', for a fee of 200 marks per annum. 'Warwick was to serve with two esquires and six yeomen and to support the prince against all but the king, in England or abroad; when so required, he was to serve with a larger retinue, on which occasion he and his men would be at the Crown's wages.'[9]

Henry could now only wait for his father's death. He was convinced of the justice of the English Crown's claim to Aquitaine. He was, further, of the mind that the legal claim must be backed up swiftly with military force. His high sense of responsibility under God for his people – including those of his people who were French – drove his plans. He also believed that any doubts which might linger about his family's right to the throne could best be dispelled through asserting their claims in France. In a trial by battle, God would grant him vindication. During the last three years of Henry IV's reign, relationships between father and son apparently deteriorated further, culminating in the dismissal of the

---

XVII

Here shewes howe he offered in Jherusalem at our lordes sepulcre and his hermes were set up on the north side of the Temple and there they remayned many yeres after as pilgrymes that longe after come thens reported.

Richard is shown kneeling by the tomb of Jesus, presenting an offering of money to the Patriarch. Above the tomb is Richard's shield, left as evidence of his visit.

Dear sheldes holde he offered in Iherlm at our lordes sepulcre / and his Armes were set vp on the North side of the temple and there they remayned many yeres after as pilgrymes that longe after come thens reported

XVII

Der schawe how ß Baltrdam a noble lord the Soldans leutenaunt that hym
beyng at Irlin heeryng that Erle Richard was there and that he was lynyally
of blod descended of neß ßy of warrwhich whoes lyf they hadde there in
bokes of theyr language he was ioyful of hym and w⟨t⟩ greet honoure
resceyded hym / and desired hym a his mynne to dyne w⟨t⟩ hym in his owne
place And Erle richard ful manerly bethankyng hym / graunted lord
Baltrdam to com for his pleasir

XVIII

XVIII

Here shewes how Sir Baltirdam a noble lorde the Soltans lieutenaunt that tyme beyng at Jerusalem heryng that Erle Richard was there and that he was lynyally of blode descended of nole Sir Gy of Warrewik whoes lif they hadde there in bokes of their langage; he was ioyful of hym and with greet honoure resceived hym and desired hym and his mayny to dyne with hym in his owne place. And Erle Richard ful manerly behavyng hym graunted lorde Baltirdam to come for his pleasir.

This scene, and the following two which deal with the same incident, are rather puzzling, for it is not at all clear why Richard's visit to a member of the Sultan's court should be reported at such length. There is some evidence that Prince Henry was contemplating a Crusade, so perhaps Richard was doing some preliminary research on his behalf.

Prince of Wales Council in 1411, when Warwick received a financial reward from the king for his services. For the next eighteen months Richard does not figure in the affairs of state. Presumably he spent some time on his own business. We know that he was in Warwick at Whitsuntide 1411 when according to the ministers' accounts of the Collegiate Church of St Mary he and members of his household were entertained by the Dean, Thomas Yongue, for two days at a cost of £1 14s 4d. Interestingly, a fire had recently taken place in the sacristy on the South side of St Mary's, on the site of which was to be built Richard's chantry chapel after his death. Perhaps this disaster gave him the idea for the siting of his memorial.

Henry IV died on 20 March 1413 in the Jerusalem Chamber at Westminster Abbey. His son, aged twenty-six, was crowned in the same abbey twenty days later, on Passion Sunday, with Warwick, now thirty-one, prominent in the ceremony. The new Henry V wasted no time in putting his plans for France into operation. In mid-July he sent Richard Beauchamp to discuss an alliance with the duke of Burgundy, which was concluded in September. The effect of this was that

---

XIX

Here shewes howe Sir Baltirdam at that dyner in his owne place set first Erle Richardes Chapelleyn in the chief place and next hym Erle Richard he hym self being as marchall and after dyner rewarded his men with silkes and clothes of golde. And to Erle Richard he gave iij precious stones of greet valure and in secrete wise told hym that in his bert thowe he durst nat utter his concept yet he feithfully beleved as we do. Rehersyng by ordre the articles of our feith.

At the meal, Sir Baltirdam waits on Richard and his company, but the claim that Baltirdam, a close retainer of the Sultan, is Christian seems very unlikely.

Here sheweth how Baldwim at that dymer in his owne place / sat fyrst Erle
Richardes chapelleyn in the chief place / and next hym Erle Richards / he hym
self beyng as marchall / and after dyner rewarded his
men in silkes and clothes of golde And to Erle Richard
he gave ij precious stones of grett valure And in
secrete wyse tolde hym . that in his hert thowh he
durst nat utter his conceyt / yet he feithfully beleved
as we do . Reherfyng by ordre the articles of our
feith /

XIX

Here/shewes/howe on the morn Erle Richard feested ff Baldwdins men and gabe them largely of english clothe to array them in his liue after yow degrees bothe scarlet and other cloth of colours/ this doon and by a spy shedbed to ff Baldwdins/ he come to Erle Richard and seid he wolde be of his liberty, and marchal of his hall / This ff Baldwdins was cunning in many languages Erle Richard yabe hym then a gobon of blakke puke furred and after dyner they hadd great communicacion to god.

XX

XX

Here shewes howe on the morne Erle Richard feested Sir Baltirdam men and gave them largely of English clothe to array them in his liver after their degrees booth scarlet and other clothe of colour. this don and by a Spey shewed to Sir Baltirdam he come to Erle Richard and seed he would be of his livery and marshal of his hall. This Sir Baltirdam was cunnyng in many langages. Erle Richard gave hym thn a gowne of black puke furred and after dyner they hadde greet communycacion to gedre.

Baltirdam and his men are shown wearing turbans, this time being waited on by Richard, standing at the left of the table. Precisely what is meant by 'puke' is unclear, but there is a reference in the Wardrobe accounts of Edward IV to 'hosen of puke lined with cloth'.

England and Burgundy agreed not to attack one another in France, and not to interfere in campaigns against other forces which either might engage in. This gave Henry the freedom to pursue his claims against Aquitaine without fear of Burgundy's interference. A possible marriage between Henry and Charles VI's daughter Katharine (at this stage only half Henry's age) was also discussed – a plan to unite the French and English thrones which would not reach fulfilment for another eight years after many stops and starts.

Richard was appointed to the key post of Captain of Calais on 3 February 1414, and he left immediately with 29 men-at-arms, 30 mounted archers, 200 foot soldiers and 200 foot archers. He also took with him carpenters and masons to keep the defences in good order. Calais was of vital importance not only for security purposes but also because it was the busiest commercial port in northern Europe. Most of the lucrative wool export trade passed through Calais on its way from England to the continent. Richard was to receive 6s 8d per day as Captain of Calais. His knights were to receive 2s each per day, horsemen 1s, archers on horseback 8d and archers on foot 6d. These wages give some indication of the relative importance of the different forces. Despite this promise of payment, Calais was to cost Richard dearly. In 1416 he was pressing the Chancellor for

---

XXI

Howe Erle Richard came ageyn to Venus And there was worthily received of the Duke and other lordes both spirituel and temporal And al the Citee gave lovyng to God that he hadde so wele and prosperously spedde in his Jorney to the holy londe.

Richard again passes through Venice on his journey home from his pilgrimage. He is wearing a ragged cloak, the sign of a successful pilgrim.

the Erle Richard came ageyn to Venis And there was worthily resceiued of the Duke & other lordes bothe spirituel & temporel And al the frere yaue louyng to god that he hadde so wele and prosperously spedde in his Iourneye to the holy londe

XXI

XXII

XXII

Here sheweth howe Erle Richard from Venuse toke his wey to Russy Lettowe Poleyn and Spruse Westvaleand other coostes of Almayn toward Englond by suche Coostes as his Auncestry hadde labored in and specaially Erle Thomas his grauntfadre that in warre hadde taken the Kynges son of Lettowe and brought hym into Englond and christened hym at London namyng hym after hym self Thomas. And in this Jurney Erle Richard gate hym greet worship at many turnamentes and other faites of warre.

This plate shows a tournament involving four combatants, rather than the one-to-one jousts in the earlier pictures. The text summarises Richard's route home via Russia, Latvia, Poland and Germany, and repeats the story of Thomas capturing a heathen king's son and bringing him up in his own household.

---

wages for his soldiers, as well as for the £100 per year which he should have been receiving himself. By 1418 some £46,000 was owing to the garrison,[10] much of it wages which Richard had been funding out of his own resources. It is likely that much of this was never refunded to Warwick and was written off on the death of Henry in 1422.

The Beauchamp Pageants follow Richard to Calais, where he is shown kissing a cross on arrival at the dockside. They portray him as immediately taking advantage of new opportunities for proving his prowess in jousting tournaments, defeating all comers in a major competition. More importantly for the development of Henry's campaign, Richard was sent with others to represent the king before the Emperor Sigismund in the Summer of 1414 and to enlist his support for the English claims in France. Sigismund was vitally important in the war of propaganda. Although his military authority may have been negligible in this context, his moral weight was still considerable. Attending the Council of

---

XXIII

Here sheweth howe after the cummyng home of Erle Richard from the holy lande Henry the Vth then beyng kyng of Englond was secretly enfourmed of a prevey and sodeyn Insurreccion of traiterous heretikes which solenly by nyght purposed to have taken and kept the kyng undre their rule dc subiieccion and after by his auctorite to have destroied the Church of England and to slee the prelates and distribute their possessions ayenst the honor of God after their indiscrete advises and pleasire.

This scene of the Pageants does not fit the actual chronology of events. Richard returned home from his grand tour in late 1409 or early 1410, and Henry V became king in 1413. The rebellion referred to in the text is the Lollard uprising of the Summer of 1415.

Here sheweth. howe after the cumming home of the richard from the holy lande heuy the 6th then beyng king of England was secretely enformed of a pretou and sedem fisurrecion of traiterous heretikes which sodenly by nyght purposed to have taken the king hides their rule a subiecion, and after by his autorite to have destroied the church of England, and to slee the pate and distribute their possession ayenst the honer of god after their indiscrete advise and pleasure

XXIII

Here sheweth howe this victorious & noble prynce kyng Hen' the V exposed this
matter to the lordes of his Counsell / Erle Richard then beyng present / Which
for thaccomplisshment of the kyngis entent & plaisir them dressed hym self
in to his harneys, and ful cariously w good circumspacion and forsight
advertised hym self to the subduyng of the said traytours & heretikes.

XXIV

XXIV

Here sheweth howe this victorious and noble prynce Kyng Henr' the Vth opened this matier to the lordes of his Counseel Erle Richard then being present which for thaccomplisshment of the Kynges entent & pleasir therein dressed hym self in to his harneys and ful coragiously wt good circumspeccion and forsight avaunsed hym self to the subdewyng of the said traitours & heretikes.

There are two separate scenes in this plate. On the right the King is shown in a council meeting, discussing the rebellion with Richard and four other nobles. In the left hand portion, Richard is having final adjustments made to his armour before leaving to suppress the insurrection.

Constance in the winter of 1414-1415, Warwick took lodgings in 'the Painted House' in the town, close to the cathedral in which the negotiations were taking place, and remained there arguing Henry's cause until some time in the Spring of 1415. By 11 May he was in London again, and on 19 June indentures were sealed appointing him to service in Calais during the coming hostilities. Indentures were contracts of service written twice on a single piece of paper, which was then torn in two and half kept by each party. The resultant jagged edges, which could be fitted together to check their validity, looked like a bite mark, hence 'indentures'.

Alongside the diplomatic preparations, Henry had been marshalling his supplies. Among many useful lessons learned in Wales, he had seen the importance of a good control over provisions in war. Four elements were of particular importance in Henry's build-up. The first, and perhaps the most vital, was cash. Weapons and food had to be bought; wages had to be paid. He therefore set about raising money with vigour, sending commissioners throughout the country. Richard Beauchamp donated and lent considerable amounts of money to the war effort over several years. Dick Whittington, former Mayor of London and

---

XXV

Howe Erle Richard after he hadde scowred the see was made Capteyn of Caleys where he ful notably gwided al thynges undre his governaunce And when he hadde seen al his londes & sette al thyng in dewe ordre ' ye yode to Caleys where he was reuerently resceived wt precession, etc.

Richard's appointment as Captain of Calais occurred on 3 February 1414, so the author of the Pageants has this event and the Lollard rebellion in the wrong order. The Earl kneels in front of the King and receives his papers of appointment from the Lord Chancellor, Henry Beaufort, Bishop of Winchester, who stands on the King's right in a jewelled mitre.

XXVI

XXVI

Howe Erle Richard after he hadde seen his landes, & sette al thyng in deu ordre heryng of a greet gaderyng in Fraunce in asmoche as he was capteyn of Calys' he hied hym thidre hastely and was there worthely received and when that he herd that the gaderyng in Fraunce was nat appoynted to come to Caleys' he cast in his mynde to do some newe poynt of chevalry. Wheruppon he lete paynt iij pavises dE in every pavice a lady the first harpyng atte ende of a bedstede wt a grate of gold on her lifte sieve dc her knyght called the grene knyght wt a blakke quarter And he shulde be redy to Just wt eny knyght of Fraunce xij corses and ij shildes shulde be of purviance And that knyghtes lettre was sealed […]

now a wealthy merchant, lent £2,000. These two were at the top end of the scale. Further down were lesser nobles and merchants, and even individuals contributing as little as 10d. Next, Henry needed men, preferably with experience of war. The aristocracy and nobility were contracted to provide men-at-arms, yeomen and archers (these latter were to play a key role in the coming conflicts). The supply of food was also essential, especially when long sieges were planned – the winner in a siege lasting perhaps four to six months would be the one who could keep his soldiers fed. Lastly, Henry had to ensure the supply of arms. Almost from the moment of his accession in 1413 he had been purchasing bows, strings and arrows. Guns and gunstones were being manufactured in large quantities. Also on the list were materials for siege towers, scaling ladders,

XXVII

[…] wt the scale of his hermes the felde sylver a maunche gowlys.
The secund Pavys hadde a lady sittyng at a covered horde worchyng perles and on her sieve was tached a glove of place And he knyght was called Chevaler vert And his lettre was sealed wt the Armes the felde sylver and ij barres of gowles and he must just xv courses and that shulde be ij sadilles of choyes The iiijde pavys a lady sittyng in a gardeyn makyng a Chapellet And on her sieve a poleyn wt a Rivet her knyght was called Chivaler attendant And he & his felowe must renne x cours wt sharpe speres & wtout sheldys his lettre was sealed wt golde & gowles quarte a bordour of vere thies lettres were sent to the kynges Coort of Fraunce And a noon other iij frenche knyghtes received them & graunted their felowes to mete at day & place assigned.

These two plates begin a series of six which concentrate on Richard's participation in a major jousting contest, furthering his chivalrous reputation. The long introductory rubric extends over plates XXVI and XXVII. In the first, Richard is received in Calais as its new Captain, and in the second his herald presents letters of challenge at the court. The momentous events of 1415 are ignored by the chronicler in favour of detailing Richard's jousts – an indication that the Pageants are more interested in his chivalry than in his military and diplomatic career.

XXVII

XXVIII

XXVIII

Here shewes howe as it is said afore thies lettres were received To the first applied hym self a noble knyght called Sir Gerard herbawines that called hym self Sir Chevaler Rouge. to the secund answered a famous knyght Sir Hugh lavney calling hym self le chivaler Blanke and to the iijde agreed an excellent knyght called Sir Colard Fynes at a certyn day and place assigned that is to say the xijth day of Christmasse in a lawnde called the parke hedge of Gynes.

The King of France, wearing his traditional fleur-de-lys crown, receives the letters of challenge from Richard's herald, who wears a tabard bearing the Beauchamp arms.

---

battering rams, tools for breaching walls and collapsible pontoon bridges, as well as timber, rope, shovels and mining equipment for digging under walls.[11]

Before he was able to concentrate on France, however, Henry had to contend with a plot at home to unseat him from the throne. The precise nature of the conspiracy which he faced in the summer of 1415 is unclear, but it seems to have been a loose alliance between the northern anti-Lancastrian party which his father had faced in 1405 and a group of Lollards led by the veteran soldier Sir John Oldcastle. As with the Peasants' Revolt of the 1380s, Lollardy seems to have appealed especially to the returned soldiers of the Hundred Years War. Following the death of Wycliffe in 1384 his influence had continued to grow, and the movement for reform in Church and State slowly gathered momentum. Henry, supported by Richard, moved swiftly to squash the rebellion. Throughout his life, Richard was to show no sympathy for the questioning of traditional authority which was developing throughout Europe and was gradually bringing to an end

---

XXIX

Here shewes howe Erle Richard on the first day that was the xijth day of Christmasse comyng to the felde his face covered a bush of Estrich fethres on his bede his horse trapped with the Armes of oon of his Auncestres the lorde Tony. And at the iijde cours he cast to the grounde at his spere poynt behynde the horse taile the knyght called le Cheveler Rouge And then the Erle with cloos visar retorned unknown to his Pavilyon And forthwith he sent to the said knyght a fair Courser.

Richard engages in combat against the three knights anonymously, each time wearing the insignia of one of his ancestors, although we have no knowledge of 'the lorde Tony'. The King of France is at the back right of the picture, with his nobles and heralds identified by the fleur-de-lys in the stands to the right and left. Richard is on his horse in the centre, the Red Knight having been unseated. We can see the backs of the crowd at the foot of the illustration.

Here sheweth howe Erle Richard on the first day that was the xij day of Crystmasse
comyng to the feld his face couded a busfh of Estrich fethres on his hede / his hors
trapped w' the Armes of oon of his Auncestres the lord tony And at the iij course
he cast to the grounde at his spere poynt behynde the horse tuile / the knyght called
[...]eshebek[...] And then the feld w' clooe visar retorned sinknowen to his
[...]uilyon And forthw' he sent to the said knyght a fawe course[...]

XXIX

Noue Erle Richard the second day came into the felde that is to sey the morowe
after the vij day his visar cloos/ a chaplet on his basinet and a tufto of estriche
fethres alofte/ his hors trapped wt his armes of Hampstede feld y burryd of gold
and thei mette wt hym the blank knyght/ and they ran to gider and the
Erle smote vp his visar thrys/ brake his besagues and other harneys all
his apparaile subed and so wt the vicory and hym self vnknowen/ rode to his
pavilion ageyn/ and sent to this blank knyght H hugh Calvey a spere
courser.

XXX

XXX

Howe Erle Richard the second day came into the felde that is to sey the morrow after the xijth day his visar cloos a Chaplet on his basnet and a tufte of estrich fethres alofte his horse trapped with his armes of Hamslape silver ij barrys of gowlys and ther mette with hym the blank knyght and they ran to gidre and the Erle smote up his visor thries & brake his besagues and other harnys all his apparaille saved and so with the victory and hym self unknowen rode to his pavilion ageyn and sent to this blank knyght Sir Hugh Lawney a good Courser.

The second illustration in this jousting series is similar to the previous plate. The king, nobles, heralds and crowd have changed little, and Richard is similarly treated. His challenger is still on his horse, and his visor has been opened by Richard's lance, which is shown as broken, with the point stuck in the White Knight's helmet.

---

the period known as the middle ages. The earl of Warwick was a loyal conservative, who clung firmly to the certainties of the established order.

With power at home secured, all that was now needed was a fleet to transport the expeditionary force across the Channel, and by August 1415 around 1,500 vessels had been assembled in the Solent. As they sailed they were accompanied by a flight of swans, thought to be a good omen by those who observed them. Henry sailed for Harfleur, but there is no record of whether Warwick was in the fleet. We must assume that he was back in Calais, not only overseeing that part of

---

XXXI

Howe on the morrowe next folowyng that was the last day of the Justes Erle Richard came in face opyn his basnet as the day afore save the Chapellet was rich of perle dc precious stones in Gy ys armes and Beauchamps quartered and the armes also of Tony and Haunslape in his trappours. And said like as he hadde his owne persone performed the ij daies afore so with goddes grace he wolde the iijde. Then ranne he to the Chivaler now Sir Colard Fynes and every stroke he bare hym bakward to his horse bakke and then the frensshmen said he was bounde to the sadyll Wherfor he alighted there from his horse and forthwith stept up in to his sadill ageyn and so with worship rode to his pavilion and sent to Sir Colard a good Courser and fested all the people gevyng the said iij knyghtes greet rewardes and rode to Calys with greet worship.

In the final joust of the sequence, Richard reveals his identity, and wears his own arms together with those of his various ancestors. His horsemanship and strength were so great that the French accused him of cheating by being strapped to his saddle, and so to prove his integrity, he immediately dismounted. The scene ends with him presenting a horse to his challenger, as he had to the other two.

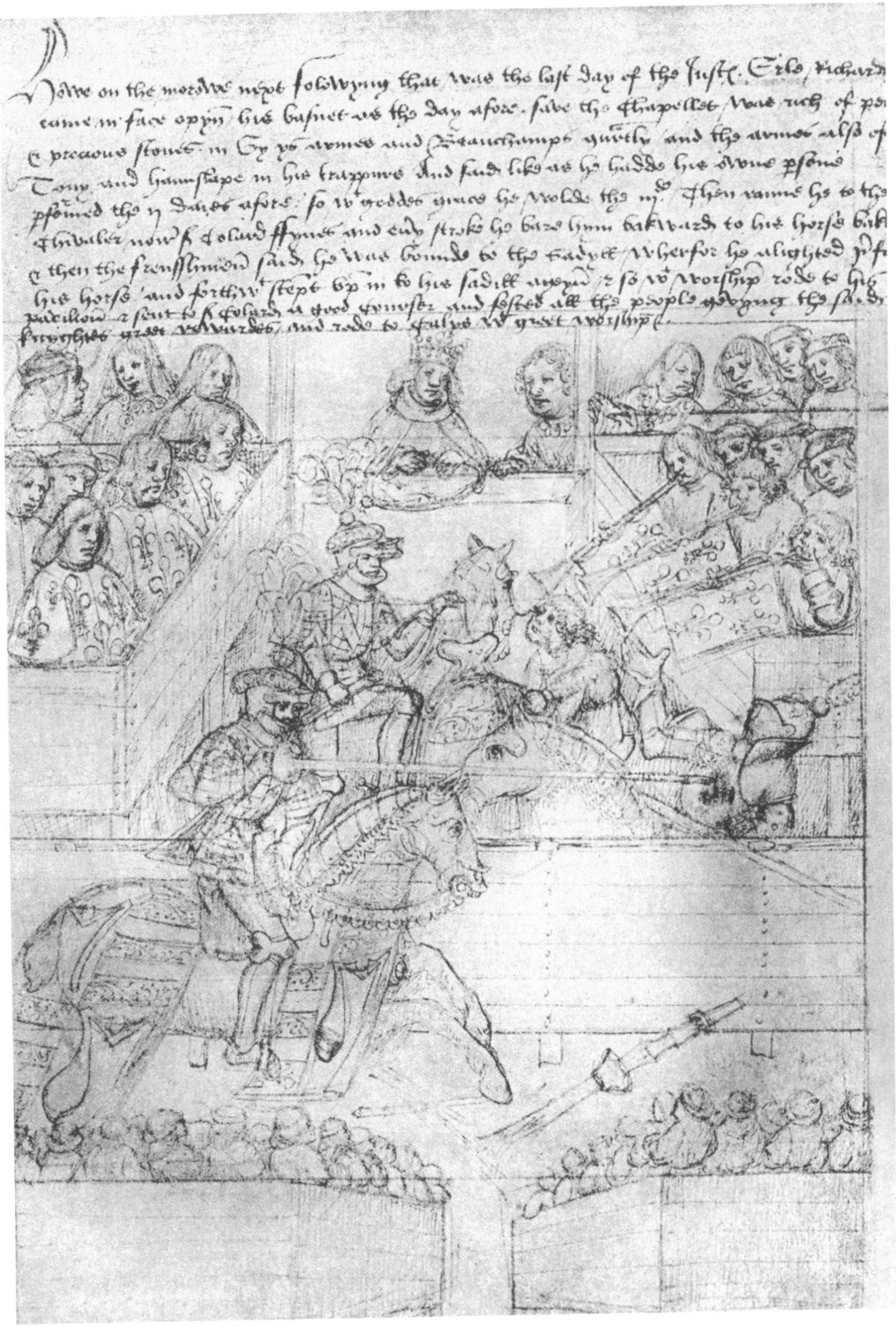

XXXI

Here shewes howe kyng Henry the v made Erle Richard and Robt Halam Busshop of Salisbury, w other worshipful Issuet his aumbassatours to the yeull counsel of Constance.

XXXII

XXXII

Here shewes howe Kyng Henry the Vth made Erle Richard and Robert Halam Bisshop of Salisbury with other worshipful persones his Ambassiatours to the general Counseil of Constance.

After the diversion of the tournament, we return to Richard's diplomatic role. Again, the chronology of the Pageants is muddled. Richard was appointed as an ambassador to the Council at Constance in October 1414. He is shown kneeling before the king, receiving his authority.

---

the Channel, but also providing a reassuring safe haven should it become necessary.

The siege of Harfleur lasted five weeks. Henry made good use of his varied stock, employing both scaling ladders and mining tools. After receiving the surrender personally, he appointed his uncle Thomas Beaufort as captain and left him in charge of a garrison of 2,000 men. Soon merchants and tradesmen from London were setting up business in a campaign to reflect the Englishness of the port. Their presence would also be useful reassurance to Henry's financial supporters, and would provide helpful cash flow back to London. The king was insistent that the townspeople were not to be ill-treated. They were his subjects, and were to be respected as such.

What would Henry do next? One obvious move was to march to Rouen, the regional capital of Normandy. It was, however, already the end of September, and the siege of Rouen would be long. Such a late start did not make sense. He had achieved his primary purpose of preventing Harfleur being used by the French as a base from which to harass English shipping in the Channel, but simply returning to England was against his nature. He decided to march to Calais, perhaps with the intention of establishing an overland route between the two English gateways to France, or maybe simply as a show of strength and possession.

XXXIII

Howe the Pope and the clergy te Emperour Sygismond and the Temporalte honorably and honestly did resceive them.

As in plate XIII, the drawing has been disfigured by adding hats and beards to the Pope and Cardinals. The Council convened in late 1414, and here Richard is shown kneeling before the Pope, who sits in a richly decorated canopy, delivering his credentials.

XXXIII

XXXIV

XXXIV

Here shewes howe a myghty Duke chalenged Erle Richard for his lady sake and he Justyng slew the Duke And then the Empresse toke the Erles lyvere a bere from aknyghtes shuldre and for greet love and favor she sette him on her shuldre then Erle Richard made oon of perle and precious stones and offered her that and she gladly and lovingly resceived hit.

There is no other record of Richard taking part in jousts during the meeting of the Council of Constance.. The Emperor Sigismund and the Empress are shown watching from a balcony. Richard, on the left of the foreground and identified by his headdress, has pierced the un-named duke's armour. The spear can be seen sticking out of his back.

———————————————————

The intended fortnight's march became drawn out by bad weather and the difficulty of crossing the Somme, the northern side of which was occupied by the French army. The battle at Agincourt on 25 October 1415 was won by a mixture of Henry's skill, torrential rain on a muddy field, and a breakdown in the French command structure. The defeat of more that 20,000 French by 6,000 English, some 5,000 of whom were archers, was the confirmation Henry craved that his title to both England and France was approved by God, and did much to strengthen his position at home. However, the massacre of unarmed prisoners on Henry's orders shows the ruthless side of his character. The way to Calais was now open, and the victorious English were there in a few days. Beauchamp rode out to meet them, accompanied by clergy carrying banners and singing the 'Te Deum', and they were led in procession to St Michael's Church in Calais for a thanksgiving service. This meeting confirms that Beauchamp had not been at Agincourt (although Shakespeare mistakenly gives him a role there) and probably not at Harfleur. He was, however, to see more than enough direct action before long.

4

Commander, Diplomat and Marriage Broker

Following Agincourt, Henry returned home for the winter, leaving Richard at Calais and Thomas Beaufort at Harfleur. He had secured his second base in France, and he had led a morale-boosting victory at Agincourt, although in territorial terms it had not advanced his aims. Apart from a naval battle off Harfleur in August, the next year (1416) was to be spent in a series of negotiations in which Beauchamp was to take a leading part. This also gave Henry time to muster his forces for a second expedition to France. Now that he had tested the opposition, he had a better idea of the resources he would need for a more extensive conquest, which would have to include the major inland cities of Normandy.

On 25 April the Emperor Sigismund, on his way to England with proposals for a compromise, was received outside Calais by Richard, who was to accompany the Emperor to his conference in London. Sigismund had brought a priceless gift for England – the heart of St George. He offered this to Richard, who diplomatically suggested that the Emperor should himself present the relic to the king on arrival in England. Sigismund spent some four months in London and Windsor, where he was instituted as a Knight of the Garter, and was impressed by the pageants and processions which were offered for his entertainment. The main business, attempting to find a settlement between England and France, was less successful, however, dragging on over the summer months. An agreement of sorts was reached at Canterbury in September when an alliance with Sigismund was signed which recognized Henry's right to pursue his claim to lands illegally held by France. The Emperor's visit from April to September had not only brought Henry the political support he needed, but had also given him time to organize his forces for the following year.

In August 1416, before the negotiations between Henry and Sigismund had concluded, French fighting vessels – carracks on hire from Genoa – were seen between Dover and Calais. Richard put to sea from Calais with a fleet of small, manoeuvrable ships, at a disadvantage in the open sea against superior fortified vessels. He managed to tempt the French ships into the Seine estuary, where the smaller English craft benefited from their mobility around the sandbanks, and the French were put to flight. The Pageants claims that Richard captured six carracks, but there is no other record of this. A storm blew up, and Warwick's ships were scattered, but he had won his first major sea battle, one of the few of the war. More importantly, he had preserved English superiority over the Channel. Richard's own ship was driven by the wind to Dover, and forced to take shelter. For a time it was feared in Calais that he had been lost at sea, but he returned safely in September in time to host a conference between Henry, Sigismund and the duke of Burgundy in October. While Henry had been talking with Sigismund in the Summer of 1416, Richard had been in France persuading Burgundy to attend the October meeting. Beauchamp's visit to Burgundy had been accompanied by 'greate feastes, playes and disports', no doubt giving him the opportunity of showing his abilities in further jousts.

The Calais conference ended successfully on 13 October with Burgundy agreeing not to oppose an English invasion of France, provided that his own territories were unmolested. Warwick accompanied Burgundy to the border of his own dominion at Gravelines and returned to Calais for the winter, while Henry crossed to England to finalize his preparations. [12]

Richard journeyed to England in the spring of 1417, probably spending some time in Warwick, for he had not been home since early 1415. His main purpose was to help Henry prepare for the summer invasion. Beauchamp had been appointed to

---

XXXV

Howe the Emperour for a special love made Erle Richard to bere his swerde and profored to geve hym seynt Georges hert Englisshmennes avowry to bryng into Englond but Erle Richard heryng the Emperor sey that he in his owne persone wolde com into Englond he by endenture restored hit to hym ageyn saiyng the Delyveryng of hit by his owne persone shulde be more acceptable & norisshyng of more love and so he did. For in short space after he come into Englond and was made Knyght of the Garter and offered up the holy hert hym self which is worshipfully kept at Wyndesore. And in his commyng and goyng at Caleys Erle Richard then beyng Capteyn there honorably resceived hym. And the Emperor said to the Kyng that no prince cristyn for wisdom nortur and manhode hadde suche a nother knyght as he hadde of therle of warrewyk adding thereto that if al curtesye were lost yet might hit be founde ageyn in hym And so ever after by the Emperors aucthoite, was called the fadre of Curteisy.

Richard's association with the bringing of St George's heart to Windsor is central to the Pageant's purpose of establishing his chivalrous pre-eminence. He certainly met the Emperor at Calais in April 1416, and accompanied him to Windsor. The intended location of this illustration is not clear – it is probably portraying the Emperor's arrival in Windsor.

XXXV

How Erle Richard in his comyng into England, wanne ij greet carryckes in the Sec.

XXXVI

XXXVI

Howe Erle Richard in his commyng into Englond wanne ij greet Carykkes in the See.

This is a lively representation of a sea battle. The ship on the left is Richard's; at the bottom right are French cross-bow men. The battle referred to is probably that which took place in August 1416 in the mouth of the Seine estury.

---

share the command of the new expedition with Henry and his brother, the duke of Clarence. In June Richard's forces were encamped around Wallopeforth, between Salisbury and Winchester, in anticipation of sailing at the end of July. The objective this time was no less than the reclamation of the whole of Normandy for the English Crown. Warwick, who for the last two years had been occupied with diplomacy and the security of the garrison at Calais, was to see serious action on French soil for the first time.

Landing without difficulty near Deauville on 1 August, Lammas day, the force of about 10,000 set out immediately for Caen. The strategy was to be a series of sieges of major cities, and the methods which Henry and Richard had refined against Glyndwr in Wales were to be used. The French countryside was dominated by regional capitals and other well fortified centres. These must be taken if Normandy was in any real sense to belong to Henry – a campaign of forays and raids into the county would be of little use if the English were not able to control the cities. Caen, the regional capital of lower Normandy, was, like Harfleur, of immense strategic importance. Lying about ten miles inland on the river Orme, it would afford another secure place of entry for supplies. It was also of immense symbolic importance, for its two abbeys had been built by William the Conqueror to house his and his wife's bodies, and the massive castle had been his Normandy base. Even today, after the devastation of the Allied Landings in June 1944, the power of the Castle and the Norman beauty of the Abbeys in Caen is apparent; in 1417 it must have been even more impressive. The walls of Caen had thirty-two towers and twelve fortified gates, and the city was surrounded by water on three sides. As with many major medieval cities there were two lines of fortification. If the city walls were taken, the inhabitants could retreat into the castle, which was even better defended than the town.

Caen was Richard's first major siege on French soil. A contemporary chronicler records that Warwick's forces were encamped around the Porte de Beauvais on the south-west of the city, while Clarence established himself to the north, on the river between the city and the sea. King Henry took over the Abbeye des Dames, the buildings in which William the Conqueror's queen, Matilda, was buried. Henry, with his usual attention to careful preparation, had brought with him not only an army but also a large entourage of craftsmen. Carpenters and blacksmiths to build siege engines; miners for tunnelling; builders and masons for bridges and towers: all were essential to the type of warfare in which the English were to engage.

Siege weapons were built on site because they had to be tailored to the context. The main destructive engines were the battering ram, by now bound with iron hoops for strength and covered by a shelter to protect the soldiers underneath, and the trebuchet, a giant catapult which hurled stones weighing several hundred pounds against the defending walls. Cannons were just coming into regular use by this stage of the Hundred Years War. They could fire balls of up to 800 pounds, and were devastating. They did, however, have disadvantages. Transporting such heavy equipment, especially over land, was slow and difficult, and the rate of fire was much slower than the trebuchet. At Caen the cannon became overheated, and had to be swabbed out with water and vinegar between shots. Over the centuries, walls had been better fortified to resist such attacks, and the castle at Caen was particularly strong.

If walls could be attacked with artillery, they could also be undermined, but mining too was a precarious business. Generally a mobile shelter, covered with wet leather to defend against burning materials being dropped from the battlements, was brought against the wall. This was known as a 'sow', presumably because the miners and soldiers underneath were reminiscent of piglets protected by their mother. Tunnels would then be dug, with pit props being erected as the mining progressed. Then, when the mining was complete, the wooden props would be set alight, the tunnels collapsed and the walls above were brought down. However, defenders could sabotage the mining activity. At Caen, they placed bowls of water on the city walls which vibrated and rippled the surface of the water as an indication of when digging was taking place underneath. Once the location of tunnels was discovered, they were filled with smoke and the bodies of dead animals were placed in them to discourage the miners with evil smells and disease.

At Caen it was eventually not the miners who were to win but an old-fashioned charge. The first attempt to cross the walls failed because the English ladders were too short, but after a siege lasting only two weeks, Richard was the first to cross the battlements, according to the Pageants, shouting, 'A Clarence, A Clarence', and planting the royal standard on the walls. The town surrendered immediately, but it looked as if the castle would resist for longer. Henry ordered that the townspeople should be rounded up, and 2,000 of them were massacred in the market place. The surrender of the castle quickly followed, and was received by Richard on 4 September 1417. As at Harfleur, London merchants were soon occupying confiscated houses and shops.

Henry stayed in Caen for the autumn and early winter, entrusting the subjugation of the remainder of western Normandy to Beauchamp. Richard spent these months in a series of smaller engagements, interspersed with talks with envoys of Charles VI which were to no avail. At the beginning of 1418 Henry was besieging Falaise, the birthplace of William the Conqueror and thus of symbolic importance, while Richard was arranging an extension of the truce with the duke of Burgundy and discussing the possibility of the Henry's marriage to Burgundy's daughter – presumably the plans for him to marry Charles VI's daughter Katharine were looking less than certain. For most of 1418, Richard continued to extend English control in western Normandy. The only significant resistance was offered by Domfront, to the south-west of Caen, which delayed him from April until July. In the end, the town was subdued by starvation, although Richard's own troops were also affected by the lack of food. As in the other sieges, Richard took hostages who were later exchanged for ransoms. This was one of the most lucrative profits of war for Warwick. While there were undoubtedly spoils of property, jewellery, precious metals, arms, cloth, and even cash to be had when a city fell, the most money was made by capturing noblemen who were shipped back to Calais or England, later to be traded for money. During the whole of the French campaigns, England's castles received a stream of these hostages. We know that four hostages were held in Warwick Castle in 1418, possibly from Caen or Domfront, for the accounts detail the purchase of shoes for them. The most illustrious hostage of the period, the duke of Orléans himself, taken at Agincourt, was to spend more than twenty years in the Tower of London.

Normandy would not be truly in English control until Rouen was captured. The capital of the region, it was the centre for justice, the seat of the archbishop and the home of the mint. It was at the time one of the largest towns in France, with a population approaching 70,000. Also, the keep of Rouen castle was the traditional

---

XXXVII

Howe Erle Richard in the warres of Fraunce toke Denfront and entred first into Cane but inasmoche as he was there with & undre lorde Thomas Duc of Clarence the Kynges next brother he sette on the walle the Kynges hermes and the Dukes and made crye a Clarence a Clarence. And then entered the Duke and gave the Erle many greet thankes. After the Erle beseged Caudebek on the water of Sayn and they appointed to stonde undre the fourme of Roon and then brought he up vessels by water to Roon And than by his policy it was beseged both by londe and water. After he wan Mount seynt Mighell and many other stronge townes And the kyng made hym Erle of Aumarle.

The text here and in the next five plates gives an accurate summary of Richard's actions during 1417 to 1420, suggesting that the chronicler had access to an reliable source. The only inaccuracy is that Mont St Michel was not captured as is claimed. This plate and the siege of Rouen which follows are perhaps the fullest and most interesting illustrations in the series, showing armour, weaponry and battlements in great detail.

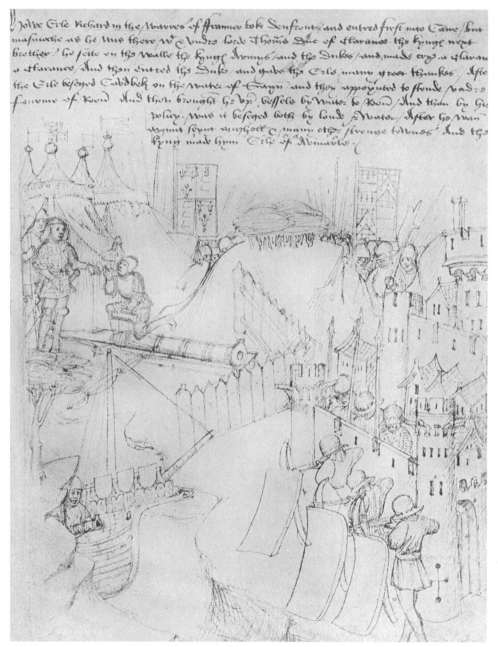

XXXVII

XXXVIII

Howe Erle Richard was atte sege of Ron there set first between the Kynges tent and seynt Kateryns And when seynt Kateryns was wonne he was sette to kepe Port Martevyle.

The siege of Rouen, which lasted from August 1418 to January 1419, was the most important set-piece siege of the campaign. The upper part of the illustration shows the town with its walls, towers and drawbridge leading to the river crossing. On the bottom right Richard is shown in armour outside his tent, and on the left he is kneeling before the King, perhaps receiving the lordship of Aumarle.

---

headquarters of the duke of Normandy – a title which Henry coveted for himself. He knew that Rouen would require a long siege. The English took up their positions overnight, and on 1 August 1418 the townspeople awoke to find themselves surrounded by five fortified encampments, linked to each other by trenches. The timing was important. Mounting a siege just before the harvest meant that food stocks in the city were at their lowest, and the attacking army could help themselves to food from the surrounding fields. There were, of course, disadvantages for the beseigers in this tactic – they had to endure the autumn rain, and perhaps the winter cold, in their temporary quarters. At Rouen Warwick commanded the south-east sector, on the bank of the Seine towards Paris. The danger of reinforcements arriving from Paris by river must have been real, and to guard against it wooden piles linked by chains were driven into the riverbed five miles upstream from Rouen.

The English supply line encountered a problem in the shape of the town of Caudebeck, 'a strong town standyng by the river of Seyne', which, located halfway between Rouen and the sea at Harfleur, was preventing ships from passing upstream. Warwick was sent by Henry to solve the problem. The town was not particularly well fortified, although its inhabitants were causing disruption to the shipping, and after only six days Richard had subdued the place, allowing more than 100 English ships immediately to sail up the river to keep the army equipped. Henry had shown his confidence in Richard's ability by sending messages to London requesting extra ships and supplies four days before Beauchamp set out for Caudebeck. The English occupied Caudebeck for the next twenty-five years, building two fortified towers, the bases of which still exist. They also installed two stained glass windows in the twelfth-century church – a clear indication that they intended to stay.

Rouen, with six kilometres of walls, was so well fortified that starvation was the only effective weapon, and Henry could use this safe in the knowledge that Warwick's action had ensured his army's own supplies. The English also cut off part of the city's water supply, and contaminated the remaining wells with dead animals;

before long the plague took hold, with bodies being piled in the streets and left to rot. As the siege lengthened and the attackers grew more frustrated, so the 'dirty tricks' increased. Animal and human bodies were thrown into the city by the trebuchets; sacking was burnt to set up smoke screens; a detachment of English soldiers dressed as French and rode towards the gates, setting up false hopes of relief. Conditions for the inhabitants were atrocious. John Page, an Englishman present at the siege, describes how the time came when the French soldiers had to eat their own horses, and then 'they were reduced to eating dogs, cats, mice and rats, and finally to any vegetable peelings they could find – they even ate dock roots.' Page reported that within the city a mouse could be sold for 6d and a rat for 30d. In December the defending troops threw 12,000 'useless mouths' out of the walls, but Henry refused to allow them to escape, confining them to the town ditch. 'One might see wandering here and there children of two or three years old begging for bread since their parents were dead. These wretched people had only sodden soil under them and lay there crying for food – some expiring, some unable to open their eyes and not even breathing, others as thin as twigs.'[13]

Rouen was hoping for relief from the duke of Burgundy, and in December 1418 his troops were in the area. That he did not come to the city's aid is probably due to a conference held between Warwick and the duke's envoys at Pont de l'Arche, at which Richard no doubt reminded them of the pacts made at Calais in October 1416. With any possibility of relief gone, Rouen's resistance crumbled early in the new year, and the inhabitants called out to Warwick that they wished to treat. Richard received a group of the towns leaders in his tent, and surrender finally came on 19 January 1419, Henry riding into his newly acquired capital of Normandy the next day.

With the capital having fallen, remaining resistance in Normandy collapsed, most towns surrendering without a fight as soon as English troops appeared. Apart from mopping-up operations, the only place offering serious difficulty to the English was La Roche Guyon, a fortress perched high on an outcrop above a bend in the Seine halfway between Rouen and Paris. Guy of La Roche Guyon, Chamberlain of King Charles VI, had been killed at Agincourt, and his widow, Perrette, refused to give up

---

XXXIX

Here shewes howe kyng henry from Roon sent Erle Richard to the kyng of Fraunce and the Erle of kyme with hym in the beginning of May with a Ml men of hermes for the marriage of Dame kateryn doughter of the said kyng of Fraunce.

The Pageants are surprisingly accurate about the dating here, for it was indeed early May 1419 when Richard re-started the process of brokering Henry's marriage to Katharine. On the left, Richard receives a letter from King Henry, and on the right he is seen riding away with his entourage.

Her shewes howe kyng Henr. from / kam sent Erle Richard, to the kyng of ffrannce
and the Erle of hys is hym, in the begynnyng of may .w a ij, men of Armes
for the mariage of Dame Kathrin doughter of the said kyng of ffrannce

XXXIX

the town and castle. From the quay at La Roche Guyon there is a clear view along the Seine in both directions, and control of it was necessary if the waterway from Rouen to Paris were to be used. The Norman keep still sits on the top of a limestone cliff, perhaps 300ft above the river. Below the keep, the château was considerabely extended in the seventeenth and eighteenth centuries. The soft rock enables tunneling to take place easily, and many rooms are cut into the cliff face behind the château façade. The setting appears impregnable, and was chosen by Rommel as his Normandy headquarters in 1944. Because of the steepness of the cliff face and the castle walls, ladders and siege engines were unusable, and mining and starvation were the only options. The two-month siege came to an end in May 1419 when Warwick's forces enlarged the caves used for storing wine in the cliffs under the castle, and cut a stairway running through the rock in order to burst through into the keep. Henry now controlled all of Normandy and was within thirty five miles of Paris. He was able to reward his commanders and other nobles for their efforts. Beauchamp was made Count of Aumarle on 19 May 1419, a title of which he was clearly proud, for he uses it alongside his earldom of Warwick to describe himself in his will written almost twenty years later.

Negotiations once again took over from fighting, and throughout 1419 they stuttered on and off. In late February Richard was involved in a series of talks with the French in Rouen, but there was no useful outcome. In March he met envoys from the Dauphin, Charles VI's son, who feared that his inheritance was about to be lost, stolen either by the English or the Burgundians. Warwick was then engaged for two months in engineering a tri-partite meeting for May, at which Henry would meet with Burgundy and Charles VI, his queen Isabeau and Katharine their daughter, with whom marriage was again on the agenda. While travelling to Provins to discuss the meeting with the French royal family, Warwick and his armed guard of around forty were attacked by a band of the Dauphin's supporters, whose aim seemed to be to wreck the negotiations. The Pageants shows a lively battle scene,

---

XL

Howe the Dolphyn of Fraunce leide in the wey vml men of hermes with the Erles of Vandon dc Lymosyn and both the pennsh Erles were slayn and ijml of his men taken and slayn all ther put to flight And Erle Richard slewe onn the said Erles his owne handes.

This incident certainly happened in May 1419, although the figures in the text of 5,000 men with the Dauphin, 2,000 of whom were killed, is probably an exaggeration. Richard's standard is on the extreme left, and the French are shown fleeing, one of whom has been hit in the bottom with an arrow. The French banner has been left blank; was the artist running short of time, or did he not know the appropriate arms?

XL

XLI

Howe Erle Richard his enemyes overcome did his message to the Kyng of Fraunce and brought answere ageyn to Kyng harries greet pleasir.

On the left Richard continues his mission at the head of his armed entourage; on the right he delivers the message to the King of France. Notice the stork nesting on the top of the tower – an omen of fertility.

---

although its assertion that Richard and his men killed 2,000 French including two earls seems unlikely. Despite being heavily outnumbered, Warwick survived the attack, but not without loosing his baggage and several horses.

At the end of May the meeting, postponed from the 15th, finally took place. On a field near Meulan, not far from Pontoise, Richard had the area marked out with plots for each of the parties, and a separate section on which a tent for negotiating was pitched. It did not augur well for these talks when the French party, including the Queen and Katharine, appeared without Charles VI. He was 'indisposed' – whether suffering from another of his bouts of madness or simply unable to face discussions about the dismemberment of his country we do not know. Speaking in French, Richard acted as master of ceremonies. The English position was that they had come to discuss peace, and that French recognition of the rights of Henry and his heirs to the provisions of the 1360 treaty of Brétigny and the dukedom of Normandy would bring hostilities to an end. Unsurprisingly, the French would not accept these terms. The stance of the duke of Burgundy in all this was unclear, and when he failed to turn up for a further meeting on 3 July is was obvious that the Meulan talks were at a close without having reached a conclusion.

Richard made several attempts to revive the discussions, but the only talks making any progress were those between Burgundy and the Dauphin. At last they seemed to recognize that their divisions were allowing Henry to have his will in France, and they reached an agreement that neither would conclude a treaty with the English without the permission of the other. This agreement was not to last for long. On 10 September Burgundy and the Dauphin met to plan joint action against the English, and the duke was killed by one of the Dauphin's attendants. The French parties were now more divided than ever, and in the resulting chaos Henry announced that he was no longer content with Aquitaine and Normandy; he now concluded that the only hope for stability in France was that he should himself be king. Warwick's task was to bring this aim to fulfilment.

The new duke of Burgundy, Philip 'the Good' (his father had been known as 'John the Fearless') received Richard and his entourage of 500 courteously at St Quentin, and negotiations lasted from the end of September 1419 until Christmas.

XLII

XLII

Howe the noble Erle Richard brought answere to Kyng henry of his message doon to the Kyng of Fraunce for the mariage of Dame Keteryn his doughter.

There are again two scenes in this illustration. On the lower level Richard, on the extreme right is being greeted on his successful mission; on the upper level he presents the King of France's reply to Henry.

The young Philip was no match for Warwick's political acumen and experience, and on Christmas day the general outlines of the treaty were agreed. The terms which Philip had accepted fulfilled all Henry's criteria, and promised to bring an end to hostilities in France. Henry would become king on the death of Charles VI, who would remain monarch in name only until his death, with Henry acting as regent. Charles's daughter Katharine would marry Henry, with no dowry being paid (Henry was said to have accepted France as the dowry). Their children would be heirs to the thrones of both England and France. Burgundy would abide by the terms of the treaty and agreed not to intervene militarily. The treaty was signed by Henry and Queen Isabeau (Charles again being too unwell to attend) on 21 May 1420 in Troyes Cathedral, and at the same ceremony Henry and Katherine were betrothed.

Katharine was still only eighteen; Henry was almost thirty-four. On their meeting the day before the betrothal Georges Chastellain, squire to Philip the Good, and eyewitness as a boy, described how Henry approached his bride to be, 'bowed very low, and then kissed her with great joy.'[14] They were married on 2 June, and the illustration in the Pageants shows them rather touchingly holding hands before the bishop, with their supporting aristocracy on either side. By contrast, neither of Richard's own marriages are portrayed in the Pageants, and it is only in the genealogies at the end that they are mentioned.

Despite the Troyes agreement and the marriage that sealed it, Warwick could not yet rest. Although the treaty had been agreed by Henry, Burgundy and Charles VI, the Dauphin whose inheritance had been given away by his father still had his supporters, and pockets of resistance to the new English/Burgundian alliance

---

XLIII

Here shewes howe Kyng henry the Vth was solempnely married to Dame Kateryn the Kynges doughter of Fraunce.

The marriage took place on 2 June 1420 in Troyes Cathedral. Richard is not specifically identified.

95

XLIII

1 *The alabaster tomb of Thomas Beauchamp, Richard's grandfather, in the chancel of St Mary's, Warwick.*

2 *The head of the effigy, resting on a pillow supported by an angel.*

3 The brass of Thomas Beauchamp, Richard's father, on the wall of the south transept at St Mary's. Originally this brass was on his table tomb.

4 Guy's Tower, Warwick Castle, built by Thomas Beauchamp in the early 1390s.

5 *The walls of Caen Castle, besieged by Richard in 1417.*

6 *The south face of Warwick Castle, built by Richard in the mid-1430s and restored by Fulke Grenville, earl of Warwick, in the early seventeenth century.*

7 *The abbey church of St Ouen in Rouen, in the grounds of which Joan of Arc recanted in May 1431.*

8 The exterior of the Beauchamp Chapel at St Mary's Warwick, built to house Richard's body.

9 The Beauchamp tomb. Also visible is the tomb of Ambrose Dudley, earl of Warwick in the late sixteenth century.

10 This view of Richard's tomb clearly shows the 'hearse', a metal cage which supported a tapestry or velevet cloth. This was removed only when mass was said in his memory.

11 & 12 *Side views of Richard's effigy clearly show his hands, with their fine naturalistic veining, in an open position of prayer.*

13 Between his hands, the Richard gazes directly up at the figure of Mary, crowned Queen of Heaven.

14 On the south side of the tomb, Richard Neville, 'the Kingmaker' is featured as a weeper. These gilt figures showed relatives or associates of the deceased.

15 Behind Beauchamp's tomb, the west wall of the chapel is painted with a 'doom', showing damned souls being led down to hell.

16 The so-called 'Doom painting', revealing Hell in all its agonies.

17 On the east wall of the chapel, a large stained glass window is surrounded by elaborately painted figures of saints and angels.

18 Detail of St Katherine and angels from the chapel's east wall.

19 & 20 These historic photographs show the figures of St Winifred (left) and St John of Bridlington, from the east window of the Beauchamp chapel.

21 The angel orchestra from the tracery on the south window of the Beauchamp chapel.

22 Angels hold a fifteenth-century hymn to Mary in the tracery of the south window of the Beauchamp chapel.

23 As a whole, the Beauchamp chapel is a masterpiece of medieval craftsmanship, featuring sublime examples of sculpture, woodwork, metalwork and stained glass – a fitting memorial to medieval England's greatest knight.

included areas of Paris. Two days after the wedding, Henry left Troyes with Philip and Warwick to head towards the capital. They quickly captured Sens, which offered only token defence, and moved on to take Monterau, a symbolic Dauphinist stronghold, for it was there that John of Burgundy had been murdered ten months earlier. As Henry moved closer to Paris, Melun was a tougher proposition. The siege here took four months, with Warwick again in charge of tunnelling. The plan was to dig beneath the foundations of the town, securing the tunnels with wooden props. The attackers would then set fire to the props, causing the collapse of the tunnels and bringing down the walls above. The problem at Melun was that the water table was high, and the tunnellers worked with mud and water up to their knees. This made the success of the operation of burning the props very unlikely. The town's defenders broke into the tunnels and fought hand to hand with Warwick and his men in the dark. Even Henry is reported to have been underground crossing swords with Barbazan the enemy commander.[15]

With Melun taken, there was nothing between the English and Paris. In the event the capital was to offer no resistance, and within hours of arriving the English troops had control of the Dauphinist strongholds. The French Parliament endorsed the treaty of Troyes, and helpfully disinherited the Dauphin for his murder of John of Burgundy.

Warwick spent Christmas 1420 in Paris with Henry and Charles, and they were joined by a party of nobles from England. During the festivities, plans were made to return to England. The reason given was for the coronation of Katharine, and to allow the people of England to see their new queen. Henry had two other things in mind – anti-Lancastrian feeling was again stirring, and he needed to raise both money and men to secure his grip on France. He left Paris with Warwick on 27 December. They rode via Rouen and Calais, arriving at Dover on 1 February 1421. Richard was on English soil for the first time since July 1417.

5

Securing the Dual Monarchy

On 23 February 1421 Katharine was crowned Queen of England in Westminster Abbey, with Richard Beauchamp acting as Steward, as he had at the coronation of her husband. Henry immediately took her on a tour of the country. One of his aims was to raise finance by showing his success in the French wars. He had severe debts; but he also had the crown of France in his pocket. Beauchamp himself was owed a considerable sum: in December 1421 Parliament was told that Warwick and his retinue were due £28,618 13s 10d for their service in Calais.[16]

On this profile-raising journey – Henry was heading for the Welsh borders, seeking to recruit soldiers experienced in the Glyndwr campaigns – Richard accompanied the royal couple as far as Bristol and then stopped off to join his wife Elisabeth at Berkeley Castle. He arrived at the castle for supper on Monday 3 March, and stayed for exactly two weeks. It is remarkable that for this period we possess parallel household records from Berkeley Castle and Warwick Castle, enabling us to pinpoint with a high degree of accuracy the movements of the earl and his family, their guests at meals, and even their menus. The Berkeley accounts run from October 1420 to September 1421, and those at Warwick cover Michaelmas (29 September) 1420 to March 1421 and March 1422 to Easter 1423.

Elisabeth was living at Berkeley Castle rather than Warwick as a way of staking her claim to her inheritance.[17] She was the only child of Thomas, Lord Berkele, (1368-1417), and his wife, Margaret de Lisle. Eliabeth had inherited some twenty-three de Lisle manors from her mother, including estates in Wiltshire, Berkshire, Northamptonshire and the South-west, but her right to the massive Berkeley inheritance was challenged by her cousin James. The cause of the problem seems to have been that Lord Berkeley was less than clear about his wishes before he died. He promised the whole of his estates to Richard and Elizabeth, but later promised part of the same estates to his nephew James. He tried to offer a compromise, but only succeeded in confusing matters even further.[18] Beginning in 1417, the Berkeley problem was to be a continual irritation to Richard and was to become the longest running law suit in English legal history, for it was to last until 1609. The Warwick accounts record payments to messengers travelling between Elisabeth, Richard's Council in London, and the earl himself in France. That Richard was away at war did not mean that he was out of touch with his affairs at home. His advisors and officials often crossed the Channel to Calais and Rouen to keep him informed and to take instructions not only about the progress of the Berkeley case, but also about the whole range of his considerable business affairs. In 1420 he had given orders for Berkeley Castle to be forcibly taken, and for Elisabeth to be installed there. The Beauchamps had gained their great wealth not only through war and royal service, but also by marrying well; Richard was not likely to let the Berkeley fortune slip through his fingers.

The accounts give details of the ordering of the household for each day. First is a list of guests, including total numbers fed, which shows the amount of movement in the household. Most Sundays the local vicar is on the list, and there is often a passing nun or pilgrim. Then there are records of purchases, and items taken from the stores. Provisions used are listed under Pantry (bread); Buttery (wine and ale); Kitchen (fish and meat); Wardrobe (spices, wax for candles); and Marshalsea (provisions for horses and transport. On most days there is an amount for 'oblation', presumably Elisabeth's donation to charity which may have been given to beggars at the gate. Each time a new barrel of wine or herring was opened from the store, a small drawing appears in the margin of the account – a quick way of keeping track of the provisions as they were used.

A typical day was the fourth Sunday in Lent, 1421, the day before Richard arrived bringing with him six henchmen, his retainer Sir William Mountfort, nine grooms and an escort of sixty others. The absence of meat from the menu is due to the household observing the Lenten fast, when only fish was allowed.

> There came to dinner; the vicar of the Church with one clerk. Item, Bracebridge. Item, Gylbart. Item, Frankby. Item, Philpot Chamburleyn. Item, William Ferrore. Item, 2 charcoalburners. Item, 2 valets of Portbury. Item, 2 pilgrims at the gate. Item Katherine Candelmaker. To supper; Thomas Stafford with 3 valets. Item, the parish clerk. Item, 2 merchants of Bristol with 2 grooms.

> Breakfast 10
> Dinner 46   Total 94
> Supper 38

> Pantry: consumed 146 large white loaves from supply. Buttery: consumed $10\frac{1}{2}$ gallons of red wine from supply, whence issued for the chamber $5\frac{1}{2}$ gallons and for the kitchen 1 quart. Item, 68 gallons of ale from supply, whence in drinks and liveries, 22 gallons. Kitchen: Consumed, 100 white herrings from supply. Item, 80 red herrings from supply. Item 8 hardfish from supply. Item, 6 saltfish from supply. And 12 haddocks bought 7d. And in 300 oysters bought 9d. All consumed. Wardrobe. Consumed, spices, wax,

and 4lbs of candles of Paris from supply. Marshalsea. Consumed, hay for 17 horses and 4 hackneys, and I provender for the same, 7 bushels. 1½ pecks of oats, from supply.

In the lady's oblation 1d.

That ninety-four people could eat 196 fish and 300 oysters together with 146 large loaves, besides drinking roughly a bottle of wine and six pints of ale each, is astonishing to the modern mind. There were, however, probably almost no fruit or vegetables consumed, especially at this time of year, and potatoes had yet to be imported from the New World. This may be contrasted with the accounts from Rouen Castle a decade later, where there seems to be an interesting variety of vegetables and fruit on the menu.

Richard had been with his family only a matter of days when he was summoned back to London to prepare for the Parliament which would meet at the beginning of May. He left for his Essex manor at Walthamstow on 17 March. He often preferred to stay here rather than in central London, as the risks from plague were lower outside the city. Elisabeth and their three daughters followed on 28 March, accompanied by a retinue of 32 people, 57 horses and 11 carriages. Supplies followed, and four servants were paid to drive 11 oxen and 122 sheep from Berkeley to Walthamstow; Lent had now ended and meat was on the menu once more. Elisabeth joined her husband after a journey taking thirteen days, although travel was not necessarily so leisurely. In June, she was recalled to Gloucestershire on urgent business and rode there in 2½ days, accompanied by John Throckmorton, Richard's closest advisor in his home affairs. Why she returned with such haste is not recorded – we can only assume her legal saga demanded her immediate presence.

While her husband returned to France, Elisabeth travelled to Warwick, and then to Salwarpe, Richard's Worcestershire birthplace and one of the family's favourite residences. The Warwick accounts record that 3s 4d was paid for a groom to lead Elizabeth's tame bear to Salwarpe from Walthamstow.

If the Berkeley accounts give us interesting domestic detail, and even a little amusement over food and other provisions, the Warwick accounts provide insight into Richard's business affairs. The 27ft long parchment covering 1420-1421 is closely written on both sides, and furnishes a considerable amount of information. During this year, Richard received a revenue of £2918 2s 11d from his estates; but this was far from his total income. He also received royal annuities – £250 per year from his retention by Henry in 1411 and a salary as Captain of Calais, although the latter seems always to have been paid very late, if at all. In addition, there were unknown amounts from the spoils of war and ransomed prisoners, and the income from his wife's estates.

He employed a close inner group of advisers to administer his interests under his receiver-general John Baynsham, the writer of the accounts. These were generally drawn from the local Warwickshire gentry. Typical was Thomas Hugford, a squire of Emscote – now absorbed as a suburb of Warwick, but then a distinct village.[19] Hugford is referred to a number of times in these accounts, and was later to become under-sheriff of Worcestershire and then an executor of Richard's will, a good example of Beauchamp's long-term commitment to those he employed. In this he was not unlike the king, for whom relationships formed in the Welsh campaigns were to last for the rest of his life. John Verney, who became Richard's receiver-general in 1430, was already in the earl's service in the period covered by these accounts, and was to be rewarded with ecclesiastical preferments. In 1428 he became Prebendary of Lichfield and in 1432 Dean, and was also made Archdeacon of Worcester in 1438.

Also in Richard's employ were auditors, who travelled to his distant manors and estates to inspect the accounts and collect the income, and a large number of lawyers. These were retained not only for the Berkeley inheritance dispute, but also for the continuous stream of lesser disagreements among landowners and tenants under Beauchamp's influence. Richard's officials were able to arbitrate on many of these without recourse to the courts. Warwick Castle held its own unofficial 'court' every Wednesday to settle local disputes. Beauchamp also kept a council in London, again mainly comprising of lawyers, to oversee his legal interests, and maintained advocates in each of the London legal courts. This council met five times in 1420 – 21, and all the meetings were concerned with the Berkeley case. Both Baynsham and Throckmorton travelled to France more than once in 1421 to consult Richard.

Expenses for the year are also listed. There are donations to ecclesiastical institutions such as the Franciscan houses at Aylesbury and Warwick and the Dominicans at Dunstable. One pound is given to St Mary's Warwick for making a new stall; 13s 4d is paid to William, the chaplain of Guys Cliffe in Warwick, for fetching a female recluse from Winchester for Richard to consult in London. We are not told the subject of the consultation, but Richard seems to have had an interest in the pronouncements of female sages – the Pageants record him consulting Emma Raughton of York. Wages for his officials amount to £250, but payment to his London tailor is £787. This may be connected with the absence of any expenses for clothing in the Berkeley accounts for the same period, and the residence of his wife and daughters in London for the whole of the summer of 1421. There is also the astonishing sum of £107 to Mark Guydon, a merchant, for a piece of velvet cloth worked with gold.

When Beauchamp next returned to England he was to take more direct responsibility for his affairs, but for now he was required again in France. After a stay of only twenty weeks in England, Richard left on 18 May 1421 to join Henry on what was to be the king's last expedition. The regions of Picardy and Artois accepted English authority at some point during the summer, and the only substantial Dauphinist stronghold west of Paris was now Dreux. This siege lasted a month and on 18 August Beauchamp took the royal standard into the town. The army then moved on to Meaux, about thirty miles east of Paris, which was now the largest Dauphinist stronghold near the capital. Henry surrounded the town on 6 October, with Richard commanding the troops on the south of the town, across the river Marne, and keeping in touch with the rest of the army by means of a bridge of boats lashed together. Rain, cold, dysentery and bursting river banks all hampered the English, the latter washing away the improvised bridge and cutting off Beauchamp's section of the army from the king's forces. The inhabitants defended stubbornly, and Richard's cousin the earl of Worcester died when a rock was dropped on his head from the battlements. In the midst of all this, news was received that Katharine had given birth to a son at Windsor on 6 December. The Beauchamp Pageants shows the scene with the new-born infant wrapped in swaddling clothes and wearing a crown, as is his mother, still in bed and looking exhausted by her labour. Henry was never to see his heir, for when Katharine visited her husband in France the following year, the young Henry was left at home.

Henry became increasingly exasperated at the insolence as well as the resistance of the people of Meaux. Early in 1422, a donkey was taken onto the walls, and beaten until it brayed loudly, at which the inhabitants called out to the English that this was their king. He was particularly incensed by a trumpeter named Orace who blew raspberries with his instrument from the tower, and Henry made sure that the offender was publicly executed in the market square when the siege ended. [20] Harsh terms were agreed by the defenders with Warwick and Exeter in May 1422, and reputedly there were great riches to be had by the besiegers, as well as over 100 prisoners who were taken for ransom.

The siege of Meaux had left Henry exhausted, and probably not a little demoralized. Warwick continued mopping-up operations, taking Gamanches and St Valery on the Somme in June. St Valery lies on the mouth of the Somme where the river is too wide for a crossing, but protects a sheltered basin on the estuary. The long quay was a useful port and access point to the region, and the small castle commanded clear views across the vast flat expanses of the Somme. Between St Valery and Gamanches is the small village of Beauchamps – perhaps the place from which Richard's ancestors originated, and through which he must have passed. Today it is a rather unattractive industrialized village of about 5,000 people. Richard was quickly subduing the northern border of Normandy, where little serious opposition was offered, but was soon called from Cosne, where he was leading a relief for Philip of Burgundy, to the king's bedside in Vincennes, about ten miles south-east of Paris. The long siege at Meux had taken a heavy toll on Henry, and he had not fully recovered from its rigours. He probably contracted dysentery there, although whether this was the final cause of his death is not known. Warwick and Exeter were both with Henry for his last days, and there was much discussion of the future, the position in

---

XLIV

Howe kyng henry the vjth was born at Wyndsore on seynt Nicholas day the yere of our lorde MCCCCXX

Henry VI was actually born on 6 December 1421, not 1420 as suggested in the text. Katharine is shown wearing her crown in bed, and the infant, wrapped in swaddling cloths, also wears a crown.

XLIV

XLV

XLV

Here shewes howe accordyng to the last Wille of kyng henry the Vth Erle Richard by the auctorite of the hole parliament was maister to kyng Henry the vjth And so he contynowed til the yong kyng was xvj yere of age And then first by his greet labour he was discharged.

It is rather surprising that the deathbed of Henry V is not shown, and the Pageants move swiftly to Richard's service to Henry VI. The picture shows Richard taking up his charge in Parliament, with the lords temporal on the left and the lords spiritual on the right.

France and the arrangements for the minority rule of his eight-month-old son, soon to become Henry VI. Henry said that if he had wronged anyone, which he did not believe, he asked pardon. He thanked Warwick and Exeter for their services, which he said he would have more suitably rewarded had he lived longer, and instructed them to continue the campaign in France until the provisions of the Treaty of Troyes were fulfilled.

The Pageants claims that Henry gave instructions on his deathbed that Richard should be 'Maister' to his son, although this does not appear in his written wills or codicils, and Beauchamp does not seem to have acted in that role until given it by the Privy Council in 1428. Indeed, the codicil to Henry's 1421 will, added on 26 August 1422, gives Humphrey of Gloucester the general oversight and protection of the heir, with Exeter to be responsible for his education. There is, however, one piece of independent corroboration to the Pageants' assertion, for the contemporary Burgundian chronicler Monstrelet also records that Beauchamp was given the guardianship of the baby prince on Henry V's deathbed. It is not, therefore, beyond possibility that the Pageant is correct, and that Henry's dying wish was for Richard to have oversight of the new king's upbringing.

Henry V died in the early hours of Monday 31 August 1422, in the month of his thirty sixth birthday. Not since Richard the Lionheart in 1199 had a king died outside England, and this was to be only one factor in the confusion which was to ensue when the news reached England. His body was taken to London via Rouen, where it rested for sixteen days. Beauchamp, who had spent so much of the preceding two decades on the battlefield with his king and friend, accompanied the body home.

Whatever the rights and wrongs of Henry's claim to the crown of France, his decade of clear and purposeful leadership had united the country to a degree which had not been possible for half a century. He was clearly a man of exceptional talent and energy, although whether he would have seemed so able a ruler in peacetime as he was in war is debatable. He valued loyalty very highly, especially among the inner circle of senior military leaders who had been close to him since the Welsh campaigns. In all this, Richard Beauchamp excelled. His strategic ability, personal bravery and sound council, together with his absolute and unquestioning support of the Lancastrian cause in general and Henry V in particular, placed him at the very centre of power.

6

The Infant King

While Richard was arranging the return of Henry V's body to his homeland, news that the king had died was causing confusion in England. It was not even known in Westminster that Henry was ill, so when his death was announced on about 7 September (for it took a week for the fastest messenger to travel from Paris to London), there was a great sense of shock. His son, now Henry VI, became the youngest monarch ever to sit on the English throne. A mere baby, it would be many years before he could take any part in government. The problem was compounded by Charles VI of France not yet having died. He was to survive Henry by only six weeks, but this complicated the provisions of the treaty of Troyes, was unforeseen in Henry V's will, and made the transfer of power much more difficult. His son had not yet been born when Henry wrote his will in 1421 and a codicil added a few days before his death gave responsibility for England to the duke of Gloucester and for France to the duke of Bedford, Henry's two younger brothers. There was, however, a lack of clarity in his intention, which was to sow the seed of dissent and struggle in the Council. At the end of August 1422 roughly half the earls and dukes of England were in France with the king. Those left were either too old to fight, or too young, being in their early teens or in one or two cases young children. The skeleton Council which met in mid-September made temporary provision for government until the full Council could meet after Henry V's funeral, which took place in Westminster Abbey on 7 November.

The full Council of seventeen members met for the first time in December 1422, and in the same month, although we do not know the precise date, Richard's wife Elisabeth died. The Council contained a good mix of the generations: six were over fifty and five under thirty. Richard Beauchamp, at exactly forty, was in the middle. They were a capable and experienced group of men most of whom, like Richard, had been with the late king throughout his French campaigns. Over the ensuing years, Warwick and Gloucester were present at most meetings of the Council, other members being less regular. Their guiding principle was to continue the policies of Henry V, so that they could hand on an intact inheritance to his son when he became old enough to take the reigns of power himself. Warwick was in a strong position, for not only had he been close to Henry in France and in Wales but he had also played the leading part in negotiating the treaty of Troyes. If anyone understood the intentions underlying the dual monarchy provisions of the treaty, it was Beauchamp. From the outset, however, there were tensions. The main cause was lack of clarity over the position of the duke of Gloucester, who interpreted his dead brother's will to mean that he should have sole power in England during his nephew's minority. Bishop Beaufort of Winchester, an associate of Beauchamp, was appointed Chancellor in July 1424, and Beaufort's clash with Gloucester was explosive. Their conflict was to undermine the authority of the Council for the next decade, and to lead to policies which were later shown to be disastrous.

The financing of Calais was to be a running sore for Beauchamp, and was to be one of the main topics of discussion for the first year of the Council. In March he was arguing for the payment of his own wages, and for pay to his soldiers which was now more than two years overdue. This was a symptom of a deeper problem – the Council's commitment to Calais and to English superiority in the Channel was less firm than at any time in the previous ten years. They decided to run down Henry's fleet, not only because it was costing too much to retain, but also because they no longer saw a need for it as Normandy had been secured and Henry VI had inherited the crown of France. This was perhaps the biggest single mistake made in the 1420s, and was to play a large part in the reversals in English fortunes at the end of that decade.

In 1423 Warwick was re-appointed as Captain of Calais – we would be justified in assuming that he took the post somewhat reluctantly in view of the financial losses it had caused him – and was also appointed Captain of Rouen. He now controlled not only the major crossing point between England and France but also the seat of English power in Normandy. The next five years were to see him dividing his time fairly equally between France and England. In France, Bedford was continuing his brother's policy of completing the conquest of Normandy and securing the French crown, which Bedford now believed belonged rightfully to his nephew. In June 1423 Beauchamp led an expedition of 1,600 men with the purpose of securing the northern border of Normandy, which he achieved by the autumn. Before long, Normandy was no longer regarded as the front line, and Bedford was able to re-establish a more normal civilian administrative structure. The borders were under the command of Salisbury, Suffolk and Warwick, with the latter having control of the south and east – the most sensitive and vulnerable sectors, for any threat from the Dauphin (now calling himself Charles VII) would come from that direction. Throughout 1426 Warwick besieged castles in Maine, pushing steadily towards the symbolic stronghold of Orléans, the duke of which was still in the Tower of London. Richard was given the title of Lieutenant General in Normandy, Anjou and Maine late in 1425, thus giving him ultimate authority whenever Bedford was in England on Council business.

Richard recognized the value of propaganda and was actively engaged in spreading the message of Henry's right to the dual crown. The Beauchamp family had patronized the poet John Lydgate in the past, and both they and the Crown were to do so increasingly in the 1430s. In July 1426 Richard commissioned Lydgate to produce a translation of the poem 'On the English Title to the Crown of France' with an illustrated genealogy, the original of which was hanging on the wall in Notre Dame Cathedral in Paris. In the 1430s and 1440s many copies of this poem were circulating in England, a number of which still exist.

> *Verily, liche as ye may se,*
> *The pee-degre doth hit specifie,*
> *The figure, lo, of the genelagye,*
> *How that God lost for her purchase*
> *Thurgh his power and benigne grace,*
> *An heir of peas by iust successioun,*
> *This ffigure makith clere demonstracioun,*
> *Ageins which noman may maligne,*
> *But he that stondith in the veray ligne,*
> *As ye may se, as descendid is*
> *Of the stok and blode of Seint Lowys;*
> *Of which we aught of equite and right*
> *In oure hertis to be glad and light,*
> *That we may se with euery circumstaince*
> *Direct the lyne of Englond and of Fraunce.*

Beauchamp was clear that propaganda and military action belonged together if his aims were to be achieved. In the first week of 1427 he took Pontorson, an important point on the supply route for Mont St Michel, the offshore fortress still held by the French and never to be conquered by the English. An eyewitness reported that all the inhabitants of Pontorson fought doggedly, and that an elderly nun was seen on the ramparts pushing a ladder away from the walls, injuring two of Richard's men who were climbing it at the time. A few months later, the siege at Montargis was less successful, and may have been the beginning of the reversal of English fortunes. Beauchamp was joined in this siege by the earl of Suffolk and his forces. Under cover of darkness, the French attacked a section commanded by Sir John de la Pole, Suffolk's brother. His negligence in posting a proper watch led to 1,500 English soldiers being killed or wounded. Richard tried valiantly to rally the forces, but they had no alternative but to retreat, abandoning their artillery. In commemoration of this ignominy the town of Montargis instituted a festival on 5 September known as the 'Fête aux Anglais'. On this date annually their victory was celebrated and Beauchamp's captured banner was paraded through the town, a tradition continuing until 1792, in which year the banner was burned.

Later the same year, Richard was relieved of the captaincy of Calais and replaced by Bedford. It is not clear what the reasoning behind this move was; surely it could not have been due to the untypical losses at Montargis. Perhaps the Council had heard enough of Beauchamp's grumbles about the cost of keeping the garrison at Calais and the money owed to him; perhaps there were some who felt that he was becoming too powerful in France, with the captaincy of Rouen and the lieutenancy of Normandy now added to his responsibilities. Whatever the reason, Richard was beside himself with rage. He was still furious a year later when, inspecting Calais' fortifications, he ranted at several of Bedford's retainers, describing them as the 'cause principal of his offence'. Bedford tried to pacify him by paying off his debts, but the Council was told that the total annual income of Calais would not clear the amounts owed.[21]

The earl of Warwick was obviously disillusioned with France, and decided to return home. Perhaps illness was also contributory to his leaving – he spent two months ill in bed in St Albans, the only recorded instance of him being unwell. For his service in France over the previous five years, he was rewarded by the Council with the Lordship of Châteaulevant and its castle and surrounding land.

During these years, Richard had not been in France continuously as he had in earlier campaigns, and seems to have been as active in England in personal and government affairs as he was across the Channel. On 29 March 1424, for instance, he and the Bishop of Worcester were instructed by the Council to raise money from the citizens of Coventry 'for the continuation of the present war in our kingdom of France.' In this period there seems to have been a surprising burst of literary activity by the Beauchamp family, perhaps stimulated by their close acquaintance with John Lydgate, and also by marriages within the family. In 1423-4 both Margaret, Richard's eldest daughter, and Richard himself were to marry. Margaret, and her husband Lord Talbot, were each given a richly illustrated Book of Hours, both of which still exist. These were made in the renowned illustrative workshops in Rouen, almost certainly at the request of Richard himself, and the newly married couple are portrayed on the front cover of each volume. Margaret herself later commissioned Lydgate to write a legendary poem about Guy of Warwick, the Beauchamp's heroic ancestor.

Having contracted an excellent marriage in terms of property to Elisabeth, (although the problem of the Berkeley inheritance was still far from settled), Richard continued the family tradition when he was widowed in December 1422. By the time Elisabeth died, he was over forty, with three daughters and no son. It was therefore imperative that he should marry again quickly, for failure to produce a male heir would mean that his estates would be divided between his three daughters, and the fortune which the Beauchamps had amassed over centuries would be dissipated. Fortunately, Warwick's cousin, Richard Beauchamp of Worcester, had recently died, leaving as his widow Isabel, who was heir to the vast Despenser estates. Medieval dowagers who were both rich and young did not remain unmarried for long, and on 26 November 1423 Richard married Isabel at Hanley Castle. Isabel was to bear Richard the male heir which Elizabeth had not given him – Henry was born on 22 March 1425 – and another daughter, Anne, who was born in September 1426. Anne survived until 1492, and was to play an important role both in national politics and in commissioning historical propaganda fifty years later.

From this period in the mid-1420s also comes the only piece of literature which is claimed to have been written by Richard himself. Preserved in the library of John Shirley, Richard's secretary and later a significant collector of literature, it is a poem written for Isabel, presumably sent to her from France, for it expresses her husband's distress at their separation. We know that Richard himself possessed at least two books of poetry. A copy of *Poesies* by the French writer Jehan Froissart, inscribed on the flyleaf 'Se livre est a Richert le gentil conte de Warrewyck' is still held in the Bibliotheque Nationale in Paris. Although the poem written by Richard is not directly taken from this book, there are a number of similar pieces which may have served as models for it. Isabel herself commissioned John Lydgate to write 'Fifteen Woes of Our Lady', a book of devotion to the Virgin Mary.

Ballade made of Isabelle Countesse of Warr & Lady Despencer by Richard Beauchamp Eorlle of Warrwyk

I can not half the woo compleyne
that dothe my woful hart streyne
with bisy thought and grevous peyne
whan I not see

my fayre lady whose beaute
so fully presented is in me
that I for wo in adversite
may not astert

from hir good list that never thwert
I shall knowe sore that me smert
but right humbelly with lowly hert
hir ordenaunce

obey and in hir governaunce
set al my welfare and plesaunce
abyding tyme of allegeaunce
and never swerve

til that the dette myn hart kerve
for lever is me hir man to sterve
than any other for to serve
for her noblesse

her flouryng youthe in lustynesse
grownded in vertuous humblesse
causeth that she cleped is mystresse
I yow ensure

of all good chance and aventure
that may be given by nature
til any worldly creature
for she alloone

in vertue is and ther hathe noon
thus seyne bothe summe and evreyche oon
that deal with her and end in oon
preyse hir maner

Her wommanhed hir lusty chere
so wold God my lady dere
at my request and my preyer
your list to rue

on me hir man that hole and truwe
have been and chaunged for no nuwe
ne never wol myn hert remuwe
from hir servyce

and that is myn hertis empryse
beseching hir that in some wise
she wol for my guerson avyse
and wommanly

counsayled by pitous mercy
resceyve me that heyvyly
endure thus and pytously
in to hir grace

and whyles that I have lyves space
out of myn hert to arrace
the discomfort that me manasse
dothe in my thought

but of she ther of nothing rought
and I be lytell worth or nought
hir wommanhed certes ought
and gentylesse

to ruwe upon myn hevynesse
for hir to serve in stedfastnesse
myn hert and al my busynesse
have I give

for ever more whyles that I lyve

In other ways 1425 was a less good year for Richard. An interim settlement in the Berkeley dispute, probably prompted by Gloucester, temporarily gave half the inheritance each to Warwick and Lord James Berkeley. Richard received five manors, including his first wife's favourite residence of Wotton-under-Edge in Gloucestershire, and rents in many of the other Berkeley manors and hundreds. Richard was deeply dissatisfied by this compromise, and it did little to improve relationships with Gloucester, already strained because of the latter's pretensions to absolute power in the Council.

In the same year, members of Richard's household were involved in another inheritance dispute. Lady Abergaveny was the surviving wife of Richard's uncle William, younger brother of his father. While she was still alive, the lordship and lands of Abergavenny belonged to the dowager; and on her death they would revert to Richard. She stubbornly stayed alive until 1435, and had a reputation for cantankerousness. In November 1425 Lord John Talbot, Richard's son-in-law, and several of Richard's circle fought a pitched battle with members of the Abergavenny household at the dowager's manor of Snitterfield, only about ten miles from Warwick. Whether Beauchamp had taken any initiative in arranging this raid is unknown. What is known is that Lady Abergavenny's men were hauled before the courts, whereas Richard was able to prevent his own followers from being indicted.[22]

Another dispute of the same year also undermined Beauchamp's prestige at Council. On 15th May 1425 Lord Mowbray, claiming descent from Edward I, again asserted his precedence at court over Warwick, resurrecting a quarrel which went back almost two decades and had subsided while Warwick spent most of his time in France. Sir Walter Beauchamp, Richard's cousin and also a member of Council, reminded them that in 1414 Henry V had placed Beauchamp not only above Mowbray, but also above the king's own uncle. As a compromise, Mowbray asked for, and was granted, his grandfather's title of duke of Norfolk, and thus gained his precedence.[23] To us this appears a sterile and childish dispute, diverting attention from the real issues of war and government. For leading aristocracy at the time, however, it was extremely serious. Status, influence in government and personal dignity had long been bound up with order of precedence at Court. The closest modern parallel is the Cabinet reshuffle, which is watched carefully to see who is moved up a place or down a place as an indication of rising or falling political favour. Taken together with his loss of the captaincy of Calais eighteen months later (although in the meantime he had gained the lieutenancy of Normandy), this manoeuvring suggests that in the middle of the 1420s Richard's stock was in danger of declining; perhaps his closeness to Henry V was resented by some members of the Council.

Before long, however, he was firmly at the centre of power as the young king's tutor. What exactly led to Richard's prominent role in the upbringing of Henry VI is unclear. The *Pageants* claims that he was given the role in Henry V's will, and pictures Beauchamp tenderly carrying the crowned infant while holding a sealed parchment, presumably meant to be the will itself. However, this is simply not true, as there is no mention of Warwick in the will of 1421 or in the codicils added in Vincennes. There remains the possibility, suggested by some, that the dying king relayed his wishes orally, but this is far from certain.

For the first seven years of his life, the infant king was surrounded by women, as was usual in contemporary aristocratic households. It may not be a coincidence that this female entourage was headed by Lady Alice Botiller (also often spelt Butler), a relative of Richard. Also in the young Henry's circle were his mother (still only in her twenties, and reputedly having an affair with Owen Tudor) and sons of earls and Lords who were his approximate contemporaries, present either because their fathers were serving in France or because they were wards of the crown after their fathers' deaths on active service. Richard's own son Henry, four years the king's junior, was to spend much of his own childhood at court and became a close friend of the king, especially in their teenage years. The main place of royal residence was Windsor, renovated just before Henry's birth, although time was spent both at the royal palace at Eltham and at Westminster when ceremonial occasions required the king's presence. Before long, however, Henry needed a male role model. Being king almost from birth meant that he had no chance to observe a monarch at work, and no possibility of learning from his father the necessary tasks of war, government and decision making which were to occupy his life. Richard Beauchamp, the person who had been closest to his father was appointed to fulfil this role.

In early May 1428, Beauchamp was already being referred to a the king's 'maister', although the formal appointment as royal tutor was not made until 1 June. In March of that year, Henry had been described as having grown 'in person, wit and understanding', and it was thought that he was now ready to be removed from his female entourage and have his upbringing overseen by a man. It may be that the appointment of Warwick, whose reputation and wealth gave him a high measure of independence, was at least in part made to protect Henry from the rivalries in the Council among those who were seeking to control him. That he was generally thought of not only as a highly experienced soldier and diplomat but also as 'the best nurtured man in England' would not have been irrelevant.

The Council minutes firstly enjoin the 'seuretee of the Kyng's persone' on Richard, and then commit his general upbringing and education to the earl. He is to 'exhorte and lerne the Kyng to love, worship and drede God', and to provide him with 'mirrours and examples of tymes passed' as role models to compensate for the loss of his father. Warwick is to oversee his literary education 'and make hym to be taught nurture, letture, langage and other mannere of cunnyng', and is given 'auctorite and power to chastise the Kyng when the Kyng trespasseth.' Finally, the new tutor is given discretion over the king's associates and household, and permission to move him to a safe place in case of 'pestilence' (the plague or other serious contagious illness) or other dangers.

Beauchamp was diligent about his duties for the next nine years, living in close proximity to the king for all this time. He immediately appointed bodyguards and tutors well-known to himself, many of whom were members of his own family. Sir William Beauchamp was put in charge of the knights who protected the boy. This may be interpreted as blatant nepotism, especially as many of them were later rewarded with various lucrative positions and pensions; but it was more likely a result of genuine concern for Henry's safety, which Richard could only guarantee if he had total confidence in those who were in the household. Later in 1428 Warwick purchased not only a primer for Henry to learn reading and religious devotion but also a made-to-measure suit of armour and two swords. We may think of these as unsuitable for a seven-year-old, but there were three essential elements in the education of the king, in common with other aristocratic boys of his age. First and foremost, he needed to be able to fight well as a chivalrous knight, in order to preserve his own life from assassination – a real threat to any medieval monarch – and to protect his inheritance. Secondly, he must be literate, and understand diplomacy and history, especially the history which led to his position as monarch of England and France. Thirdly, he should be educated in Christian piety, the stitching that held the fabric of medieval Europe together. The earl of Warwick was well qualified in all these requirements, and employed specialist tutors in each of the areas.

What can we know about the boy entrusted to Beauchamp's care at the age of $6\frac{1}{2}$ and about the new tutor's effect on the child as he grew into adolescence? Historical writing has not been kind to Henry VI, and there has been the added complication that most people view him through the lens of Shakespeare's plays. Verdicts on Henry have ranged from someone whose 'second childhood followed his first without the usual interval' (McFarlane) to a king who reigned with 'wilful incompetence and untruthfulness' (Wolffe). Described as a 'handsome, robust child who converses in French with ease' in 1434 by a Burgundian ambassador (who had no reason to embellish the truth), he was dismissed as a sickly weakling and a congenital idiot by other contemporaries. One of the few facts known about his health is that in 1453, a little over the age of thirty, he went into what seems to have been a major depressive episode for some eighteen months. This was possibly triggered by the death of Lord Talbot in battle, and the catastrophic loss of thousands of soldiers, confirming the loss of any possibility of retaining the French crown. The episode must have convinced him of his failure to live up to the expectations of the dual monarchy which had been impressed upon him in his boyhood, and would certainly have been more than enough to bring on depression in someone with that tendency. Until he recovered gradually early in 1455, he was unable to speak, and on occasion even to move.

It is probably not without significance that Henry's grandfather Charles VI also suffered from periods of madness, the symptoms of which seem to have been similar to what is now diagnosed as manic depression. There is a considerable amount of evidence that depressive illness is at least in part genetically transmitted – in gaining Katharine as his wife and guarantee of the French throne for his heirs, had Henry V also ensured that his father-in-law's madness was handed on to his son along with his crown?

Bizarrely, this same Henry VI also had a reputation for not merely Christian devotion, but even sainthood. John Rous, the Warwick historian and writer of the roll of earls and kings about a decade after Henry's death described him as 'a most holy man, shamefully expelled from his kingdom, but little given to the world and worldly affairs.' A biography commissioned by Henry VII at the end of the fifteenth century portrayed Henry VI by saying ' there was not in this world a more pure, honest and more holy creature.' Even though these may be dismissed as sycophantic attempts to re-write history in favour of the victors after the Wars of the Roses, there is still a good deal of evidence, including the views of common people who claimed miracles following his death, to support the argument in favour of Henry's genuine faith, humility and learning.

Perhaps these views of Henry are not as mutually exclusive as they have appeared. If one takes into account that he clearly exhibited symptoms of major depression in his thirties, it is unlikely that this illness had made no appearance earlier. It could well be that Henry VI was an intelligent, cultured person, mindful of his responsibilities and position, who was affected by periods of mental illness which changed his character radically and made him appear an uncommunicative fool. It is impossible to attempt a psychological reconstruction at the distance of almost six centuries, but there are some indications which might help us to understand at least in part, the riddle of Henry VI. Succeeding to the throne at the age of nine months meant that the young Henry would have been unable to remember a time when he was not king, and that he would have had no models such as his own father to observe in that role. We can only guess at how much Henry was influenced and by whom in his early years; we do know that Beauchamp was formally entrusted with that task, and so must bear at least some responsibility for the outcome.

Henry grew up war-hating, peaceful, wilful, courteous and excessively religious – hardly the most appropriate qualities for a king of a country at war in a time when rulers were expected to lead their armies in person. We may only speculate that the man who had spent the best part of the previous two decades on the battlefield with Henry V, who had fought beside him in his greatest triumphs and had argued for him in countless diplomatic missions, must have told the growing boy the stories of those events in great detail, probably many times. Perhaps placing a small child in the care of an elderly distinguished soldier was not a sensible policy. Warwick was now well into middle age for someone in the fifteenth century – forty-six when he took on the job of tutor. Not only had he lived through the 'glory days' of the conquest of Normandy, but he was now becoming disillusioned with the reverses taking place in the late 1420s. 'If only your father were still alive…' must have been a constant refrain. The damage this may have caused to the developing psychology of a small boy, especially one with a possible genetic tendency towards mental illness, can only be imagined.

On 6 November 1429, a month before his eighth birthday, Beauchamp took Henry to Westminster Abbey for his coronation as King of England. Two recent events in France had led to hasty preparations for this ceremony becoming necessary. The first was the appearance of Joan of Arc on 29 April that year, and the subsequent gains made by French forces in the Loire Valley. The tide of the war in France was turning against the English, and some significant measures would be necessary. The second was the crowning of the Dauphin as Charles VII in Rheims, the traditional place of coronation for French kings, on 18 July. England was now at a disadvantage in the propaganda war, and Richard proposed to reclaim the initiative by having Henry crowned King of France in Paris. It was unthinkable that this should take place without his first having been

---

XLVI

Here shewes howe Kyng henry the vjth beyng in his tendre age was crowned Kyng of Englond at Westm with greet solempnyte.

The Pageants now move quickly through the last decade of Richard's life, covering eleven years in only five illustrations. Henry's English Coronation took place in Westminster Abbey on 6 November 1429. The illustration shows the sceptre in his right hand and the orb in his left – the reverse of the correct positions. The two bishops standing on the step are holding the crown, its weight being too great for the eight-year-old boy.

Here sheweth howe kyng henry the vjth kyng in his tendur age was crowned kyng of Englond at westm^r wt greet solempnyte

XLVI

crowned in his own country, so arrangements were quickly made for this to happen before setting out for France. As was traditional the night before the coronations, new knights were made. These included Warwick's son Henry Beauchamp, aged only four, who was made a Knight of the Bath, as his father had been on the eve of the coronation of Henry V.

Beauchamp took Henry to the Abbey 'in his arms', although it is not clear why an eight-year-old needed to be carried. He did, however, walk out between the bishops of Durham and Bath, with Richard carrying his train. St Edward's crown, when placed upon his head, was so heavy, according to the picture in the Pageants, that it had to be supported by a bishop. An observer described Henry as looking 'sad and wise' at the ceremony. He was anointed with reputedly miraculous oil contained in a golden flask said to have come from Thomas Beckett, and French elements were contained in the rites to reflect the duality of the monarchy being laid upon the child. In the streets several people were crushed to death by the crowds, and a number of pickpockets were apprehended and had their ears cut off as punishment.[24] The courses of the banquet which followed were punctuated with huge pastry creations which depicted scenes from French history and mythology – another symbol that this was but the first part of a double coronation.

In the spring of 1430 Beauchamp took his young charge to France for a visit that was to last almost two years. They arrived in Calais on St George's day, April 23.

7

A Coronation and a Burning

Throughout 1429 and 1430 the English suffered a series of reversals in France. The nature of the war had changed, for Bedford and his forces were now defending rather than attacking, and retaining land in a country in which many of the population were hostile to the occupying force became increasingly difficult. Orléans, a key Dauphinist stronghold and crossing on the Loire, was besieged in October 1428, but the English soon suffered a severe blow to morale when the commander, Lord Salisbury, was killed by a stray cannon shot. By the end of February 1429 the besieging force had made no progress. The French were making efforts to reinforce the garrison, and Bedford, still in charge of the English effort in France, was depleting the defences of towns further north to bolster the siege. Sir John Fastolf (suggested by some as the model for Shakespeare's Falstaff) headed a contingent of 1,500 men with food supplies – mostly barrels of salted herring since Lent was starting. When this party was attacked by French troops, the resulting skirmish became known as the Battle of the Herrings. The siege of Orléans had reached stalemate by March.

The spring of 1429 saw Joan of Arc burst onto the scene. In an enigma which has never been fully explained this seventeen year old girl, dressed as a man, was able to turn around the French fortunes. In their first encounter, at Chinon, she persuaded Charles VII to let her lead his armies to relieve Orléans, then after further gains took him to Rheims for coronation in the cathedral – the traditional place for the crowning of French kings – on 17 July 1429. This act gave a huge boost of morale to the French forces, and the remaining months of 1429 saw many areas being re-captured by them. By October, the duke of Bedford had to withdraw from Paris to Rouen. Tension in the Council back in England was running high, as Gloucester was placing the blame for the reversals on Bedford's mismanagement.

It was against this background that the Council decided on the dual coronation of Henry, and after the first ceremony at Westminster Abbey, Beauchamp set off for France with his young charge in April 1430. The force taken to protect the king and to reclaim his French territories was as large as that led by his father in 1415. The folly of running down Henry V's fleet was becoming apparent, for it was difficult to assemble enough ships to accomplish the crossing. Half the Council stayed in England with Gloucester, and the remainder went to France with Henry, including Norfolk, Huntingdon, Stafford and Beaufort. The physical distance between the two halves of the Council was not the only problem which they were to face – there were also mounting disagreements about policy. The king's great-uncle Beaufort, whose presence was necessary because as Bishop of Winchester he was to perform the coronation in Paris, asserted that he would only accompany the expedition if the senior members of the Council would stop quarrelling with one another. Warwick, Norfolk and Huntingdon had to swear in Gloucester's presence that any disputes between them would be taken to the Council for arbitration.[25] On arriving in France, the entourage spent more than two months in Calais until Beauchamp was satisfied that the king's safety could be guaranteed before moving on to Rouen. They were to stay in the English headquarters in Normandy for eighteen months until it was safe enough to take Henry to Paris.

English fortunes seem to have taken a more positive turn when in May 1430 Joan was captured by one of John of Luxembourg's men during a skirmish at Compiegne. For six months she was moved from prison to prison. John, recognizing that she was valuable to both sides was trying to negotiate a good price. Her purchase for the English was brought about by Warwick and Pierre Cauchon, the Bishop of Beauvais, who was to direct the trial for her arrest had taken place in his diocese. An eye-witness reported on the outcome of the deal:

> I saw Cauchon when he reported to the Regent (i.e. Bedford) and to Warwick upon his negotiations for buying Joan. He did not abstain from

---

XLVII

Here shewes howe kyng henry was after crowned Kyng of Fraunce at Seynt Denys besides parys. Of the which coronacion in Fraunce and also the said Erle to have the rule of his noble persone unto he were the age of xvj yeres. it was the will & ordenaunce of almyghty god as or blessed lady shewed by revelacion unto Dam Emme Rawhton Recluse at all halowes in Northgate strete of York and she said that thorowe the Reame of Englond was no personae lorde ne other like to hym in habilite of grace and true feithfulnesse. to vertuously norisshe and governe his noble personne accordyng to his Roial astate. Also she put greet commendacion by the ordenaunce of god of his greet benefytes in tyme to come of devowt commers to the place of Gye clif otherwise called Gid clyffe which in process of time shal growe to a place of greet worship. oon of the moost named in Englond.

The picture shows Henry's French coronation in December 1431, with little to distinguish it from the last plate. The majority of the text, however, is devoted to the prediction of a female recluse about the future status of Guys Cliff, the chantry endowed by Richard in Warwick. Needless to say, the prediction that it would become one of the most renowned places of worship in England was not fulfilled.

XLVII

joy, and animatedly said to them some words which I did not well understand. After which he went to confer apart with the Earl of Warwick.[26]

Joan was taken to Rouen on about 28 December 1430, and was imprisoned in the Treasury Tower of the castle. At some point Warwick offered her freedom in exchange for a promise that she would not take up arms again, but she declined. A cage had been constructed to await Joan's arrival for not only had she attempted escape at least twice so far, but the English were terrified of her powers of witchcraft. In the event, the cage was not used and she was kept in leg irons. She was in constant danger of physical and sexual assault from her gaolers, and early in her captivity at Rouen she complained to Beauchamp:

> I do not dare to take off these leggings, nor to wear them unless they are
> strongly laced. You know that my guardians have several times tried to
> do violence to me. Once even as I cried out you, Earl of Warwick, came
> at my cries to help me; and, had you not come, I should have been the
> victim of my guards.

After this, some of her guards were changed, and Richard gave a severe warning to others not to molest her. He was also concerned that she might commit suicide, and so made sure that she was constantly watched. This was obviously not out of care for Joan herself, but because he did not want her to escape a public trial and execution.

Joan's trial was to last for five months, and by a remarkable coincidence we possess two sets of records for the period. The first is the well-known and much written-about transcript of the trial itself, often giving verbatim reports of the daily proceedings. The second is the much less known and unpublished household record of Rouen Castle between 14 March 1431 and 15 March 1432 which is in Warwickshire County Records Office. The first entry in this account is for the purchase of the book in which it is written, 'For this paper bought by Duffield at Roon… together with binding – 15s.' It is tantalizing that Beauchamp is not mentioned in the trial record, and that Joan is not referred to in the household account, although she was a prisoner in the castle for a quarter of its duration and the proceedings were taking place in various rooms in the castle. However, Beauchamp's role is well documented in Joan's trial of rehabilitation which took the evidence of eye witnesses twenty-five years later, and we can reconstruct much of the part he took in the affair. In addition, at one or two points the household record does shed some circumstantial light on the trial account.

Bishop Cauchon, who was assisted in the trial by several legal and ecclesiastical assessors, was in constant contact with Beauchamp, who was not himself part of the trial because it was held under ecclesiastical jurisdiction. The charges were witchcraft and heresy and much attention focussed on Joan's assumption of male dress and on her 'voices' – apparitions of St Michael, St Catherine and St Barbara who she claimed guided her actions. (Is it entirely coincidental that these two female saints are represented in the statuary around the arches of the Beauchamp chapel in Warwick?)

The trial began in the chapel of Rouen Castle on 21 February 1431, and was soon transferred to the Great Hall, presumably for more space. The first phase was a leisurely and rambling investigation, mostly about the details of her visions. To hear voices and receive visions which were in contradiction to the teaching of the Church was seen as clear evidence of heresy, so if the inquisitors could establish that Joan's voices were unorthodox, the verdict would be clear. For a young woman, then aged about nineteen, her responses are confident, and sometimes so brave as to appear foolhardy.

> She said several times to the bishop, You say that you are my judge; consider well what you do; for in truth I am sent from God, and you are putting yourself in great peril.[27]

Richard was becoming increasingly frustrated with the slow pace of the proceedings, and more than once put pressure on Cauchon to reach a speedy conclusion. He was under no illusion about the purpose of Joan's inquisition – it was a piece of political propaganda designed to discredit the coronation of Charles VII only thinly disguised as a heresy trial. Cauchon seems to have been genuinely concerned to ensure that the trial was properly conducted. At one stage, Joan was given advice on how she should respond to accusations put to her. Beauchamp was enraged, confronting the advisor with biting insults and invectives. 'Why,' he said, 'did you this morning support that bad woman by making signs to her? Rogue. If I again see you taking trouble to help her and to warn her to her profit, I will have you thrown in the Seine.'

There was a break in the trial for almost a month when Joan became ill. She attributed the illness to eating a carp sent to her by Cauchon, although whether there was any deliberate attempt at poisoning is unclear. Warwick sent his own and the king's doctors to cure her.

> The King does not wish,   for anything in the world, that she die a natural death; for he holds her dear, having dearly bought her, and does not wish her to die except by justice and the fire.

It is unlikely that King Henry at the age of nine held any such firm view of his own, but Richard did not want the public execution for heresy to slip from his grip. On her recovery, Joan was taken to the castle dungeon and shown the torture implements in an attempt to frighten her into a confession. A few days later, on 13 May, the household account shows that there was a high level conference at Richard's dinner table. Present were the dukes of Bedford and Burgundy, John of Luxembourg, Bishop Cauchon, the Chancellor of France who had travelled from Paris and many lawyers and clerics involved in the trial. In total 267 people ate with Richard that day. The account tells us that they had strawberries and cream for dessert. We have no way of knowing the content of the discussion, but from that point events moved rapidly. The discussion must have continued, for large number dined in the great hall each day for the next two weeks.

Joan was taken to the cemetery of the Abbey Church of St Ouen, it being one of the only open spaces which could accommodate a large crowd, and an audience was needed. There, standing on a specially erected scaffold, Joan was 'preached' – a learned cleric having been imported to entreat her to repent and give up her heresies. The main content of the sermon seems to have focused on the foolishness of Charles VII, lending weight to the view that the trial was about him as much as it was about Joan. She astonished her judges by appearing to say that she accepted the authority of the Church, and that her voices had deceived her. Cauchon sentenced her to life imprisonment, and she was taken away to prison, where she put on woman's clothing. This was not Beauchamp's desired outcome; the initiative was being lost. A contemporary witness said:

> When Joan was being taken back from St Ouen to prison, the soldiers insulted her, and their officers let them do it. In fact, the English leaders were mighty indignant at the Bishop of Beauvais, because Joan had not been pronounced guilty, condemned and given up for execution. Their indignation was such that, at the moment when the bishop and the doctors returned to the castle, some of the English, saying that they had ill earned the king's money, raised their weapons to strike them. They did not strike them, however. I also heard that the Earl of Warwick complained to the bishop and the doctors. 'The king is ill-served,' he said, 'since Joan is escaping.' To which one of them replied: 'Messire, don't worry. We will certainly entrap her again.'

Whether what followed was entrapment is unknown. There certainly seem to have been some elements which strongly suggest it. Joan complained that she had again been molested by soldiers, and that a 'great English Lord' had tried to rape her. There is no suggestion that this may have been Beauchamp; Joan knew well enough who was the earl of Warwick. Four days later, she was again dressed in male clothing, which seems to have been conveniently left in a bag in her cell. On hearing this, Beauchamp immediately sent a delegation to interview her, which reported that she had again claimed to hear the voices, and that they had instructed her to resume male dress. Cauchon left the prison to report to Richard. 'Be of good heart,' he said, 'it is done.

123

She is caught this time.' The next day the verdict was passed. Joan was found guilty of heresy, although not of witchcraft, for refusing to accept the authority of the Church which proclaimed her voices to be demonic, and for persisting in wearing men's clothing – a practice 'against natural law'.

On 30 May she was taken with an armed escort of 80 English soldiers to the Vieux-Marché in the city, where scaffolds had been erected. In response to her request that she might be given a cross to hold, an English soldier made one of two pieces of wood and put it into her hand. The fire was lit, and she took some time to die because the executioner was not able to climb on the high scaffold to despatch her. As she died, the spectators heard her calling on St Michael, St Catherine and St Barbara. Her body was totally burnt, and the ashes scattered in the Seine. Some witnesses claimed to have seen doves flying away from the castle at the moment of her death.

On one level, Richard Beauchamp does not come out of this episode well. The earl of Warwick portrayed in French history and in dramas such as Shaw's *St Joan* is shown as a callous bully, insistent on securing his solution. This does not seem to sit easily with what we know of his cultured life and genuine Christian faith. Seen through Richard's eyes, his motive was to protect the young Henry VI, and to ensure that his kingdoms were handed on undamaged. Having fought beside Henry V to ensure the English claim to the French throne, it looked to be slipping away due to the propaganda victories brought on by this girl. Richard was fiercely loyal to the house of Lancaster, and deeply committed to his responsibility for Henry. From his point of view, the only way to ensure the young king's safety was to remove the threat which came from Charles VII and Joan of Arc.

The next six months were devoted to attempting to secure the coronation in Paris. Irritating claims were circulating that Joan was not dead, and that a substitute had been burned in her place. In August 1431, French forces were in the region of Beauvais accompanied by a young girl in man's armour, said to be Joan. Beauchamp mounted a raid, and routed the French force after trapping them in a pincer movement. In this action he captured Charles VII's master of horse, de Saintrailles, who would be worth a large ransom. Lord John Talbot, Richard's son-in-law, was de Saintrailles prisoner, so this capture gave hope for Talbot's release. The negotiations took until 1433, and Saintrailles was exchanged for Talbot and a large fee.

The household account gives a fascinating insight into the daily life of Rouen Castle during 1431. The document is written on 410 sheets of paper, watermarked with the fleur-de-lis. It is written in Latin, by an Englishman, Nicholas Roudy the steward, living in France. This gives rise to some difficulties with spelling, which is often phonetic. There are notes of arrivals and departures within the household, and of particular interest are the details of two journeys – the first to Paris for the coronation in December, and the second the homeward journey to Warwick early in 1432.

The six headings for each day's provisions are identical to those in the Berkeley accounts from a decade earlier. As Richard's eldest daughter Margaret was running the household for her father while her husband Talbot was held by the French, this suggests that she must have learned her account-keeping system from her mother.

Pantry is always listed first, giving the number of loaves consumed as well as details of the fruit eaten. During the year, this included apples, pears, figs, peaches, quinces, grapes cherries and nuts. The first strawberries of the year were eaten on 13 May – the day of the conference about Joan. This category also occasionally included chives and lettuce.

The next item is 'Buttlery', listing wine and beer. Surprisingly, not only French wine was consumed. White wine from the Rhine is purchased, as is vin d'Espagne (possibly sac, or sherry, a favourite drink of English noblemen). Beer was bought in barrels about once every three weeks.

The kitchen entry gives details of fish and meat, and here again the variety is astonishing. Fish was bought by the basket, and included eel, perch, plaice, ray, salmon, pike, carp, sole and herring. The latter seems to have been mostly salted and used during Lent. As might be expected in Normandy, there was also abundant seafood. Oysters, mussels, crabs and prawns were available most days. Beef was also eaten every day, and the other meats listed are mutton, veal and pork – most of the pork seems to have been used in charcuterie.

The fourth category is 'Pulletria', or poultry. This lists capons, chickens, cockerels, pigeons, plovers, woodcocks and quails. Dairy products such as milk, cheese and butter are mentioned here, as are eggs and herbs.

The next entry is wardrobe, giving details of candles and wax used. This varied according to the time of year, with 3lb of wax being used each day in June, 6lb daily in October, and 12lb in January.

The sixth and final item refers to the needs of the horses and their consumption of food and litter.

At the end of each month is a reckoning which accounts for everything used in the period, and details money spent in both French and English currency. Of interest here is the currency fluctuation, which moves by a much as 35% during the twelve months of the account, giving some indication of the economic instability caused by the war.

Each day there is a list of names of those dining. The king and his entourage were frequent visitors. Although Henry was resident in the castle for the whole of this period, he had his own quarters and household. On 27 March he brought with him 54 attendants to dinner, while the duke of York brought a further six. On that day 120 were given dinner. The castle was clearly the scene of many meetings about the progress not only of Joan's trial, but also of developments of the war in general. The dukes of Bedford, Burgundy and York, and the earl of Stafford were often present.

The order in which guests are listed in the record is puzzling. Lady Talbot heads the list each day. She was clearly heading the household for her father while her husband was held hostage by the French. After her, the list appears to be random, with the king, the dukes, and Beauchamp himself appearing in no apparent order, and often below a visiting merchant or nun. The reason for this may be that a clerk wrote down the names of diners as they entered the hall. Lady Talbot always led the party in, but after her, members of the household and guests came in at different rates, and were noted down as they entered. In the Great Hall, the tables were arranged in a large 'U' shape, with the nobles and senior guests sitting along the top, and others sitting according to rank on the side tables.

Catering must have been a real problem, for the number turning up to be fed at dinner varied between 60 and 210. Breakfast seems to have been taken only by children, often as few as five. The other meal of the day, 'prandium', usually served between 60 and 70. Guests are not listed, and it was probably only members of the immediate household who ate.

Nobles were not the only guests to be fed in the castle hall, and it is possible to follow the rhythms of the seasons by noting the tradesmen who pass through. In September and October there are grape-pickers, and in November there are furriers to prepare skins for winter clothing. Minstrels arrive on 6 June, and falconers on 21 February. On 19 November there is a marriage between two members of the household, James Dryland and Alice Lyghtfoot, and about 90 people are given dinner after the ceremony. Other domestic necessities are noted. On 20 September glasses are purchased; on 6 October kitchen utensils are repaired.

The domestic detail provided is fascinating, but it is tantalizing that the history-making events which were happening in and around Rouen Castle at the time are only hinted at obliquely. On April 4 messengers arrive from Louviers; we know from other sources that Beauchamp was just about to inaugurate a long and frustrating siege there. The security of Paris was in serious doubt during the first half of the account, and the frequent visitors from the capital must have been providing up-to-date information on the situation, while the possibility of the coronation going ahead was assessed. Joan of Arc was imprisoned not a hundred yards from where they were eating, and her trial must have been the main topic of conversation for at least three months, yet she is not mentioned once.

The one event which the account does take note of is Henry's coronation, and this is because in December 1431, the household moved to Paris.

> And in expenses of the lady Countess of Warwick going by water from Roon to Paris beginning on Saturday the first of December going by water and staying for 7 days and so to Friday on which day at night she entered Paris – with Madame Talbot, 2 damsels, 3 esquires, 1 groom, Madame Godard with 1 damsel, 1 esquire, the wife of Mr John Somerset with 1 damsel, 2 yeomen, 1 page, 4 officers of the king, 1 esquire of the cardinal with 1 yeoman, 2 armerers, with 54 persons guests for the same time.

This was clearly the movement of the women of the household. Beauchamp himself left Rouen on 20 November, taking with him an entourage of several thousand soldiers, to make sure that Paris was safe. They had waited in Rouen for eighteen months, and if the English were to capitalize on the burning of Joan, the coronation had to be achieved.

Henry entered the capital on Sunday 2 December 1431, riding a white charger and accompanied by Warwick and the dukes of Bedford and York. It was four days before Henry's tenth birthday. They were met at the gate of Paris by the bishop, together with leading representatives of the courts, the legal profession and the city's merchants, and were greatly impressed by the pageants arranged to welcome the king. At the gate of St Denis there was a huge shield bearing the arms of the city, and a silver ship carrying a crew representing the main elements of society. Three massive hearts, symbolizing the three estates of the French nation, opened to spill out doves and flowers as a welcome.[28] Tableaux presented scenes from the life of the Virgin Mary and other saints. As they moved through the city, clergy were outside their Churches displaying their collections of relics – an important part of medieval religion and piety. Of especial veneration was the arm of St George, which Henry stopped to kiss. Following this entry, Henry was taken to the castle at Vincennes, the place of his father's death to await the coronation itself.

The household account continues to record the movement for this period. To dinner on Thursday 13 December in the Beauchamps' lodgings in Paris came '32 officers of the King with tailors and skinners of the city working on the King's robes, and the laundryman.'

Throughout the time in Paris Richard did not leave the king's side. Fears for his safety were genuine, and Richard wanted to conclude the business as quickly as possible and move back to more secure territory. On Sunday 16 December, 'The lord and lady with Madame Talbot went away by reason of the King's coronation.' Richard took Henry, now just ten, to Notre Dame where on a huge platform he was crowned King of France. Lydgate recorded the feast which followed. There were three courses, each of which contained many decorative elements symbolizing the two kingships now held by the boy. These included venison 'plantid with losenges of golde'; royal custard 'with a leparde of golde sittyng theryn'; a fried leopard's head with two ostrich feathers; cold baked meats 'like a shelde quarterly redde and white, set with losenges and gilt'. How much of this decoration was edible is not recorded. An observer suggested that there were more English elements than French in the ceremony, and the same source went on to complain that, 'the food, like the organisation, was shocking; the English were again in charge, and most of it had been cooked the previous Thursday.'[29] It seems that French views of English cooking do not change.

Following the coronation banquet, Henry was taken to the French parliament, where he promised to uphold all the laws and customs of the country. He then asked Beauchamp to translate his words into French so that they could be understood by his new subjects. The party did not delay long in Paris. To Richard's great relief they left on 26 December after brief Christmas celebrations, arriving back in Rouen on 30 December, and heading home for England, arriving at Calais on 23 January 1432. Henry had now been crowned king of both countries. In theory they were united under a single monarch; in practice they were still at war. Although Henry was never to return to France, the 21 months he had spent there, culminating in the ceremony in Paris, was to leave a lasting impression. He was always to believe that he was the legitimate king of France, and the reverses suffered by his forces throughout the 1430s and '40s were to cause him great distress, and almost certainly contributed to his mental illnesses. Richard must have returned to England with his king wondering what had been achieved. The English had spent huge sums of money, purchased and executed Joan of Arc and crowned Henry, but the war had still not turned back in their favour. Indeed, it might be thought that the whole exercise caused them more damage than advantage, as calls for the canonization of Joan began to be heard.

8

Losing France – Richard's Old Age

Richard's return home to England is described in detail in the closing pages of the Rouen Castle household accounts. As the earl and countess were now on the road with their entourage and the young king, the account-keeping system accompanied them. They returned to Rouen for a fortnight, from 30 December 1431 until 12 January 1432. On that day the account states baldly, 'At Roon for breakfast and went away.' The large group, about ninety people, went via Dieppe, Abbeville and Montreuil to Calais, leaving on Saturday 9 February after 'breakfast early' and crossing to Dover on the same day, where they had dinner. The party then went in different directions. Isabel, Margaret and the women went to Canterbury on pilgrimage, and from there via Faversham and Gravesend to Walthamstow, meeting up with Richard again on 18 February. Richard and Henry went immediately to London, where Richard had much catching up to do on his business affairs, having been out of the country for more than eighteen months. On 21 February Henry made a formal entry into London, and was greeted with pageants equal to those offered in Paris. As he rode into the city, with Richard by his side, he was met by two antelopes bearing the arms of England and France. On London Bridge three allegorical empresses, Nature, Grace and Fortune, presented him with gifts. Progressing through the city, tableaux, shields, wild animals and genealogies all confirmed his status. The culmination was a service of thanksgiving in St Paul's, where the boy king was given the heavy sceptre of St Edward to bear on his shoulder as he walked into the cathedral.

Richard returned to his lodge at Walthamstow, his baggage having been taken around the coast by boat (three men were paid 16d to unload it and carry it into the house). He and his family left together at the end of February and travelled by road and barge via Staines, Windsor, Henley, Tewkesbury and Worcester to Warwick, finally arriving on the evening of 14 March – a total of 18 days to cover a journey of 195 miles, although on nine of those days they did no travelling. The tortuous nature of the route is explained by evidence that Richard spent time conducting discussions with his business managers and checking on the current affairs of his estates as he progressed towards the Midlands. John Verney, who had been in Richard's service for more than a decade and by 1430 was his receiver general, accompanied him on the return to Warwick, and spent time with him 'on questions to do with his domains.' There were some difficulties on the journey, mainly to do with Isabel's carriage, which broke down several times and had to be repaired: '4 horses hire and 3 men to help the lady's chariot by the way 14d. Also for 5 new collars with 4 pairs of traces bought by John Carter for the lady's chariot 11s. 4d.' (Monday 10 March) The final entry in the account is for 15 March 1432, the day after they arrived back in Warwick.

Richard was to spend most of the next five years in England – the longest extended period he had spent in this country since 1414 when he was first appointed to Calais. During this period his time and interests were divided fairly equally between his continuing role as Henry VI's tutor, together with oversight of the royal household and security, and his own affairs in Warwick.

Contemporary observers report that King Henry, now aged ten, was growing into a likeable and intelligent – even precocious – youth. Richard was careful about Henry's associates, and continued to build up around the household a group of people whom he could trust, many of whom had Beauchamp family connections. After the French expedition and the spectacular entry into London, Richard began to introduce Henry to more of his subjects. He spent Christmas 1433 to St George's day 1434 at Bury St Edmunds as the guest of the abbot, and Richard taught him the skills of hunting and falconry. The main reason for the length of the stay seems to have been less the abbot's open-handed generosity than the financial embarrassment of the Council and the royal household. For much of the summer of 1434 Henry and Richard were together at Kenilworth Castle, a favourite Lancastrian stronghold and summer residence and also only eight miles from Warwick, so that Richard could give time to the centre of his web of interests.

At the centre of national interest all was far from well. England and France were both economically exhausted by the war, which had now been raging without a pause for two decades. Wool prices had fallen drastically, reducing the crown's revenue to £54,000 in 1434, and tension over the conduct of the dual monarchy continued. In 1433 the young Henry begged his uncles Bedford and Gloucester to stop quarrelling about France, but the power struggles between them continued unabated. Warwick was becoming increasingly exasperated about the effects all this was having on the king, and when Bedford was abroad in France, Gloucester increasingly tried to exert his influence on Henry and the Council. Added to all this, Henry was becoming more difficult to manage and seems to have been learning to play off one faction in the royal family and Council against another. Richard saw himself as occupying a precarious position, potentially caught between the rivalries of Bedford and Gloucester and at risk of future reprisals from a growing youth who seemed to resent any restriction or correction. It was a difficult situation for the earl. Henry was not yet out of childhood, but according to the medieval theory of monarchy was the source of total authority. Richard was a mere subject, and to lay hands on the king might be interpreted as treason. He therefore returned to the Council, asking for a clear and formal indication of their support.

On 29 November 1434 Richard took a long list of demands to the Council which cover several pages in the record. His first concern is that unsuitable people are having an influence on Henry, although they are not named. He is given power to 'put them from exercise and occupacion of the Kyngs service'. Richard also reports that Henry 'is growen in yeers in stature of his persone and also in conceyte and knoweleche of his hiegh and royale auctoritee and estate.' However, there are disadvantages in the king's maturity, for 'as he groweth shul causen him more and more to grucche with chastysing and to lothe it so that it may resonably be doubted lest he wol coneyve ayenst the saide Erle,' and Warwick requests the reiterated support of the king's uncles and the Council. Their response is, 'It is agreed as it is desired.' He further complains that Henry has been diverted from his learning and 'spoken to of divers matiers not behovefull,' and requests that he or one of his own knights should be present at all interviews with the king. No doubt Richard found it useful not only to be able to censor what was being said to the king, but also to receive from his knights a full report of all conversations. The discussion ends with the Council's assurance that they will emphasize to the king their support of Richard, and that he enjoys their full support in his oversight of Henry's learning, discipline and associates.

Warwick's task was not made easier by Bedford's death in September 1435, for even while in France the king's eldest uncle had placed some restraining influence on Gloucester's thirst for power. Henry was attempting to assert even more of his own authority, and from August 1336 we can see more of his influence in government. In May 1436 Warwick was discharged from his duties as tutor, so that he could spend more time 'with his own affairs', and on 13 November 1437 the full powers of kingship were vested in the not-yet-sixteen-year-old Henry. Even at this point, the future of his reign must have looked ambiguous. He was described by a French visitor as looking 'more like a monk than a king.' He was reputedly mild-mannered and quietly spoken; the most extreme oath he used was 'forsooth and forsooth.'[30] He enjoyed reading chronicles, and had a particular interest in King Alfred, even campaigning for him to be made a saint. War and bloodshed distressed him, and his instinct was to come to a negotiated settlement with France, although he never forgot his coronation in Paris, and was convinced of his right to both crowns. Education was a personal priority of his reign, and he was later to found both Eton College and King's College, Cambridge. He was notably religious, displaying an 'obsessive and ostentatious piety' and devotion to the Virgin Mary. Any attempts to trace Beauchamp's influence on these traits must be unprofitable. Henry had an unusually strange upbringing. His father's death before he was a year old; being king for as long as he could remember; the tensions around him at court; and his education at the hands of a middle-aged legendary hero must all have contributed to his inner conflicts.

At the same time as educating the king and trying to navigate the difficult waters in the Council, Richard was attending to his own empire. He was at the head of a financial and land holding which was by the 1430s among the richest in Europe, and the records of his finances which still exist are better and more extensive than those of any other English magnate in the first half of the fifteenth century.

When Richard became earl in 1401, his income from land gave him a clear profit of about £1,400 per annum. By 1420 this had more than doubled to about £3,200, and in 1432-33 it reached £5,471. It increased even more in 1435 when the death of Lady Abergavenny brought the estates given by Richard's grandfather to his uncle William back to the main line of the family. Not all this increase was due to good management and astute investment – his two marriages had brought considerable land, and the annual income derived from Isabel's inheritance was perhaps as much as £1,250.[31] The traditional Beauchamp heartlands of Warwickshire and Worcestershire remained the core of the portfolio, and had been strengthened and extended. Richard now also held manors in Norfolk and Suffolk, Wiltshire and Berkshire, Cornwall and Devon. Only north of the Trent were his possessions small, and there the house of Lancaster was the dominent landowner.

But land was far from Richard's only, or even main, source of revenue. Since 1411 he had been retained for life by Henry V for a sum of 250 marks per annum (about £170), which continued after Henry's death. He also received fees as Captain of Calais, Captain of Rouen, member of the Council and royal tutor, along with various other offices. In addition, he collected considerable amounts from ransoms and from the other spoils of war, and all these sources more than doubled his income from land in the years 1415–1432. However, the cost of Calais was never fully repaid to Richard, and despite continuous nagging in the Council, and being given some royal jewels as surety in 1432, he died being owed over £12,000 for this service.

The income Richard received from land and that which came from other sources seem to have been kept separate. As well as his receiver-general, who kept accounts of the estates' income, Richard had a cofferer who looked after other money, which included his diplomatic and war incomes and sales of wood and mining rights. This system was mirrored in the way Richard's followers and employees were arranged, for he had almost entirely separate entourages for war expeditions and domestic affairs.

How did Richard spend his money? A major expense for noblemen was the provision of substantial marriage portions for their daughters. Richard had four daughters, and although we have no record of the precise sums paid, they would have been considerable. Securing the marriage of his first daughter, Margaret, to Lord Talbot was a shrewd move for it brought two leading families together, and Talbot would provide long-term assistance to Richard in France. Conversely, we know that in 1434 Richard Neville, the earl of Salisbury, paid 4,700 marks to obtain the hand of the nine-year-old Henry Beauchamp for his daughter, the largest marriage portion paid in the fifteenth century.

Building was also a major expense for someone of Richard's status. The Collegiate Church of St Mary in Warwick had been completed by his father, and Richard was already planning an addition to it to house his own body. Warwick Castle also benefited from his attention. The spartan fortification of his ancestors received added state rooms and private apartments, and he rebuilt the whole of the south side of the castle, giving it much the appearance which it has today. The south tower – now known as Caesar's Tower – was built by Richard, as was a large stable block. Elmley, Hanslope and Henly castles were also rebuilt by Richard, as Cardiff had been a decade earlier, and many other manors, castles and religious establishment received support. Richard also had the ambitious scheme of making the River Avon navigable up to Warwick by a series of locks and canals, which would enable boats to access the sea via Stratford, Evesham, Tewkesbury, Gloucester and Bristol. This idea would have greatly increased the trading strength of Beauchamp's estates, but never came to fruition. Interestingly, the scheme was revived in the 1990s, when a group attempted to raise support for making the upper Avon navigable, and quoted Richard Beauchamp in their support.

The Beauchamp family continued to patronize the arts as they had done in the 1420s. John Soursby, a musician employed by Richard who also worked as master of the choristers at St Mary's Warwick, composed a setting of the mass, the *Sanctus*, which still exists in a manuscript book in Aosta in Northern Italy. From these years there is also a lavishly illuminated book of hours which belonged to Richard's son Henry, now in New York. Also in this period he made a gift of a copy of Boccaccio's *Decameron* in French to Humphrey, duke of Gloucester, who was a noted collector of fine books. Whether this volume already belonged to Richard or whether he bought it specifically as a gift is not known. Was Richard making this gift to ease tensions between himself and Gloucester in the Council, or was it simply a present from one cultured nobleman to another?

The administration of such a vast enterprise required the establishment of what was effectively a private civil service. Beauchamp's closest associates were his private council and his stewards and household officials. At the centre of the estates enterprise was the receiver-general and an inner circle of officials who oversaw the working and productivity of farms and manors and collected the rents and dues. Most of these were minor gentry from Warwickshire who had been in the service of the Beauchamp family over several generations, and can be easily identified from the frequency with which they appear in the records and the number of offices they held.[32] There were several individuals and families who were employed by Richard continuously over two or three decades, and rose within his administrative structure. For example, Thomas Hugford, who held the position of Richard's receiver-general in 1435, had been preceded by his father in the same post in 1402. One of the most interesting of these officials was John Shirley, who was among Richard's retinue fighting against Glyndwr in 1403, was collecting pay for Richard's soldiers in Calais from the Council in 1414, negotiated with Lord Neville 'about a marriage' in 1422, and was being paid a pension at the time of Richard's death in 1439. Shirley is of particular importance because as Richard's secretary he had an interest in book and document collecting, and we probably owe the survival of many of the Beauchamp family documents to him. Richard rewarded those who were loyal to him well, not only with pay but also with ecclesiastical preferment. John Verney, who was receiver-general in 1430, was made Dean of Lichfield in 1432 and Archdeacon of Worcester in 1438.

Richard was not much involved in the war with France after his return to England for his primary national duty was to be with King Henry. The direction of English policy in France was increasingly unclear. Richard was present at a meeting of the Council in Calais in May 1433 at which Bedford and Gloucester took very different positions on strategy. Following the fresh impetus given to France by Joan of Arc, the English position was becoming even more insecure. Soldiers at Calais were disillusioned and threatening mutiny, and the shape of the war had changed. The major settlements having been captured under Henry V, Bedford's army was now defending rather than attacking. Sadly for the English, warfare of the period was turning in favour of the attacker, because medieval walls were not designed to withstand attack from the cannon which were now in regular use by the French. More importantly, the disunity between the French factions on which England had capitalized was coming to an end. In the autumn of 1435 Charles VII and the Burgundians formed an alliance, the immediate result of which was the recapture of Harfleur late that year.

Bedford having died in July 1434, Gloucester was able to assert a more aggressive strategy, and the largest army of the 1430s set out in 1436 under the command of the duke of York, aged twenty-five and recently appointed as Lieutenant of France to replace Bedford. Calais was besieged by the French in the summer of 1436, and the Pageant shows Beauchamp riding alongside the duke of Gloucester in its defence. This action was successful, and the Burgundian force retreated on 29 July, but by the time York's army reached Paris it had already fallen to Charles VII. Despite

---

XLVIII

Here shewes howe Philip Duc of Burgoyn beseged Calys and humpey Duc of Gloucester Richard Erle of Warrewik and humpey Erle of Stafford with a greet multitude went over the see and folowed the Duc of Burgoyn he ever fleyng before them. And there they sore noied the Contrey with fire and swerde.

The narrative has now jumped five years to the summer of 1436. The view of Calais, unlike many of the other illustrations, does bear some resemblance to reality, with the square tower of the church, which still stands, clearly dominating the centre.

In these sheres bfore Philip Duc of Burgoyn beseged Caleys / And
hunfrey Duc of Gloucest, Richard Erle of Warwyck and hunfrey
Erle of Stafford, Wt a gret multitude, went ouer the see, and folwed
the Duc of Burgoyn, he did fleyng before them, And there they sore
wend the countrey, Wt fire and swerd,

XLVIII

XLIX

successfully repelling the attack on Calais the English were losing territory monthly, and the folly of disbanding Henry V's navy was apparent after the fall of Harfleur, when control of the Channel swung back to the French. For the first time in thirty years, the English south coast was in danger of attack.[33] By late 1436 the French were close to Rouen, Richard's old home and the symbolic heartland of English power in Normandy.

In early 1437 Lord Talbot, Richard's son-in-law, was leading counter-offensives, and his military ability succeeded in recapturing a number of towns in Normandy which had recently fallen to the French. The duke of York was, however, too inexperienced to organize the administration of a country at war, and lacked strategic understanding. There was only one person who had the necessary experience, who commanded the respect of the various factions in the Council and who had the favour of the king, now taking more power to himself. Henry's role was central here. His recently retired mentor had for years told stories of how he and Henry V together had successfully conquered France and gained the crown. So in April 1437 the king appointed Richard to be his Lieutenant in France in place of the duke of York. Richard was extremely reluctant to accept the position. He was fifty-five, and beginning to enjoy retirement from national politics, which had occupied him without a break since 1410. In an age when few people lived beyond the age of fifty, and even at forty were likely to be affected by chronic illness or disability, Richard was an old man. He wrote to the king, pointing out his long service to the Crown, and begging to be excused.

> My going over at this time is ful farre from the ease of my years and from
> the continuall laboure of my person at sieges and daily occupation in the
> warre, seeing the length of tyme that I have belaboured in the service off
> nobull kings off good memory, your grandsire and fadere and about
> youre self, as well as in youre warrs as about your noble person.[34]

The teenage king, however, seeing Richard as the solution to his French problems, insisted, and Richard's sense of duty and loyalty ensured that he obeyed. All his conditions for undertaking the task were agreed by the Council, and he insisted that if they were not met, he would feel free to return home. He also managed to wring

---

XLIX

Here shewes howe Kyng henry vjth made Erle Richard his lieutenant of Fraunce and Normandy.

Richard kneels to accept the authority which he had declared himself very reluctant to take. His ship waits in the background.

some financial concessions out of the Council, including a promise of back pay still owing from Calais, although there is no evidence that it was ever received. He assembled a force of 5,320 men at Portsmouth, but took his time in departing. A bill dated 11 July 1437 for the painting of banners for his trumpeters and tapestries shows that he took with him 'xviii grete Standards entreiled with the Ragged Staff, pris the pece 12s.' Because of the virtual economic collapse of Normandy, ravaged by continuous war, Richard's men had to take food and other provisions with them. A herd of cattle was driven from Budbrooke, three miles west of Warwick, to join the fleet. On 8 August at Caversham Richard made his will.

> I will that when it liketh to God that my Soule depart out of this World, my Body be enterred within the Church Collegiate of our Lady in Warrwick where I will that in such Place as I have devised (which is known well) there be made a Chappell of our Lady, well faire and goodly built, within the middel of which Chappell I will that my Tombe be made; and in the mean time my Body to be laide in a clean Chest afore the Altar that is on the right hand of my Lord my Fathers Tombes till the time that the said Chappell and Tombe for me be made, and then my Body to be taken up and laid therein.
>
> Also, I wish that there be said every Day dureing the Worlde in the aforesaid Chappell that (with the Grace of God) shall be thus new made, three Masses, whereof one every Day of our Lady God's Mother, with Note after... The Second Mass to be every Day without Note of Requiem. The third Mass also without note to be the Sunday of the Trinity, the Monday of the Angells, the Tuesday of St Thomas of Canterbury, the Wednesday of the Holy Ghoste, the Thursday of Corpus Christi, the Fryday of the Holy Cross and Saturday of the Annunciation of our Lady. And to the observences of these Masses in wise as it is above expressed in the said Chappell during the Worlde every day to be duly said... I will that there be in all haste after my Decease and before all other things to be said for me five thousand Masses.
>
> I will that in the name of Heryott to our Lady there be given to the Church of our Lady in Warrwick myne image of Gold and of our Lady, there to abide for evermore...
>
> I will that my son Harry have the Cup of Gold with the Daunce of Men and Women...
>
> I ordayne foure Images of Golde, each of them to the wieght of twenty pounds of Golde, to be made after my Similitude or Figure with myn Armes holding an Ancre between his hands so figured and them to be offered and delivered in my Name, that is to say, one of them at the Shrine in the Church of St Albon, to the Worship of God, of our Lady

and of St Albon; another of them likewise at the Shrine of the Cathedral Church in Canterbury; the third of them in like form at Bridlington; and the fourth of them at the Shrine in the Church of St Wenefride in Shrewsbury.

Other inclusions in the will, besides the transfer of his estates to his son Henry, include annual gifts to the Dean and Canons of St Mary's Warwick and to Tewkesbury Abbey, and new houses to be built for the priests at the Chapel of Guy's Cliffe. The cost of the gifts would have been considerable. The material for the four gold statues alone would have cost in the region of £1,280 before casting and finishing. The places to receive the statues were all of significance to Richard: he had been ill in St Alban's; he received his Garter at Shrewsbury; and he held special devotion to Thomas Beckett and John of Bridlington. The 'heryott' was a feudal fine due to the lord of the manor on the death of a tenant – an assertion by Richard that he had not held his riches as of right, but on loan from Mary. The Masses to be said for his soul demonstrate his acceptance of the medieval Catholic belief in purgatory – a place in which the souls of dead Christians are cleansed of sin before their acceptance into heaven. Masses said in the person's memory were believed to shorten the time it was necessary to spend in purgatory. The most significant part of his will for us is the instruction to build a new chapel on the south side of St Mary's, properly called the Chapel of Our Lady but generally known as the Beauchamp Chapel. The site of it is not specified in the will, but is 'known well', presumably by his family and the Dean of St Mary's, and turns out to be the area damaged by fire some twenty-five years earlier.

With the forces and provisions loaded and his will made, the fleet set off for France, but the weather was atrocious and they were soon driven back by storms. Several attempts were made to cross – perhaps six aborted journeys in as many weeks – one of which almost ended in disaster. A drawing in the Pageants shows Richard and

L

Here shewes howe Erle Richard when he with his Navy took the salt water. in short space rose a grevous tempest and drofe the shippes into diverse coostes. in so moch that they al fered to be perisshed. And the noble Erle for castyng lete bynde hym self and his lady and henry his son & heir after Duc of Warrewik to the mast of the vessel to thentent that where ever they were found they myght have been buried to gedres worshipfully by the knowledge of his cote armor and other signes uppon hym but yet god preserved hem al & so retorned to Englond and after to Normandy.

This is the only illustration, apart from the genealogies at the end of the work, which portrays Richard's family – indeed until now there has been no mention of his wife and children. In the ship depicted in the upper part of the picture, Richard and his wife and son can clearly be seen strapped to the mast.

Here shewes howe Erle Richard when he w[i]t[h] his lady tok the salt water in
short space rose a tediows tempest and drofe the shippe into Swisse cost in
so mvch that they al fered to be perished / And the noble Erle for custumer
like bounde hym self and his lady and hem his sone[s] hew
after two of warre wok to the mast of the vessel to the entent
that where ever they were fownd they myght have been
buried to gedres. worshipfully by [th]e knowleg[e] of his cote
armu[r]e [th]e shypp[e]s vppon hym / but yet [th]e[n] preserued hem al
[th]er [fo] retur[n]ed to England and after two stormandy.

L

Here sheweo howe he efte from England come quietly into
Normandy / And there ad a lorde sawl the kyng lieutenaunt & gaded
which fewueo Richent in the frenshe toun / sonably and dystretely behad
hym felf / that bothe Englissh and ffrensh were glade of hym /
playnly pacdyuig by his gidyng / that god was to hym

LI

141

LI Here shewes howe he este from Englond come quietly into Normandy And there as a lorde Roial the kynges lieutenant ck governor which formes Regent in the penche tong so nably and discretely behadde hym self that bothe Englissh and Frensh were gladde of hym playnly perceivyng by his gwidyng that god was with hym.

Richard is shown sitting in state, holding a rod of office. The positive description in the text does not match the decline in English power in France which Richard was not able to halt.

Isabel and their son Henry bound to the mast of the ship which is being tossed by the storm, a coat of arms identifying them so that in the event of death they could be buried together. For those who believed in the significance of omens, it was not a good start to Richard's lieutenancy in France. The company eventually arrived in Rouen in November 1437, six month after Richard had been appointed to the role, and £24,000 was sent from England to finance the campaign for the retention of Normandy. Rouen was no longer the great medieval city it had been at the beginning of the century. The devastation caused by the English siege had not been repaired, and the place was economically depressed.

Richard found the military situation in France to be desperate. The recently established French alliance was attacking towns at will and was threatening to besiege Rouen. Warwick instituted an immediate review of the English position, took command of Rouen himself and seems rarely to have left the city. He appointed Talbot commander of the army in the field, and for the next year the French advance seems to have been stemmed. Although Talbot made few gains, he also suffered few losses, and a situation of stalemate seems to have been reached; even Richard Beauchamp could do little more than a temporary holding operation. By late 1438 he was making serious attempts at a negotiated settlement with Charles VII and Burgundy, but the French, now in a position of power, were reluctant to agree to anything less than the abandonment of English claims to French territory.

Richard's last eighteen months must have been frustrating and disappointing. The gains of the years in which he had fought alongside Henry V were slipping away.

LII

Here shewes howe by the honde of god he fil seke in the noble Cite of Roon and as a Cristyn Knyght departed from this worlde all the sacramentes of the Church devoutly of hym before Resceived the last day of May the yere of our lorde MCCCCxxxix the yere of his age lviij.

Richard is shown as tired and emaciated on his death bed. The cleric in the centre holds an open box with containers of holy oil for the last rites. The dating in the text is wrong – he died on 30 April, not May.

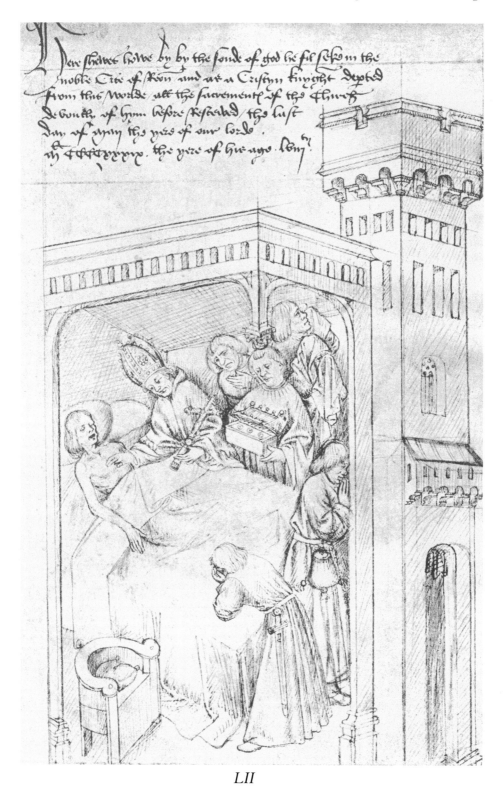

Here sheweth howe by þe sond of God he fil seke in the noble Citie of Ron and as a Cristin knyght departed from this Worlde all the sacrements of the church & vouch. of hym before reseibed / the last day of thym this yere of our lord . M CCCC lxxxix . the yere of his age lxiiij

LII

Her sheweth howe the same yere of his decesse the iiijth day of Octobr
next folowyng, his corse was honurably conveied as voie by watir &c
by londe from Roon unto Warrewick, & there worshiply buried in the
college of our lady & thomas founded by his noble Auncestres, the bisshop
of lichfeld beyng executor effray and many lordes ladyes and
other worshipful people there beyng present.

LIII

LIII

Here shewes howe the same yere of his decesse the iiijth day of October next folowyng his Cors was honorably conveied aswell by water as by londe from Roon unto Warrewik & there worshiply buried in the College of our lady Churche founded by his noble Auncestres the bisshop of lichfeld beyng executor officij and many lordes ladyes and other worshipful people there beyng present.

In the background can be seen the outlines of Warwick Castle. There is no suggestion in the picture or the text that this is a temporary burial until the new chapel is ready to receive its founder.

———————————————————

Despite his experience and courage, Richard was old, and even with Talbot as his assistant could do little to hang on to English territory in the face of a united France. His heart was no longer in the fight – it is clear from his plea to the king that he would prefer to be home in Warwick.

Richard Beauchamp died aged fifty-seven at Rouen Castle on 30 April 1439. In the Pageants he is shown on his deathbed, looking emaciated and fatigued with a bishop offering him 'all the sacrementes of the Church devoutly of hym before Resceived.' We do not know the cause of his death. Perhaps he was simply worn out by a lifetime of campaigns and responsibility. His body lay in state for some weeks in Rouen Cathedral while two of his retainers, John Nanfan and Richard Curson, settled his affairs in France. On the last day of August a memorial service was held in his honour in Rouen Cathedral, and in October his body was returned

> aswell by water as by londe from Roon unto Warrewik and there worshiply buried in the College of our lady Church founded by his noble Auncestres the bisshop of lichfield beyng executor office and many lordes ladyes and other worshipful people there beyng present.

9

The End of the Beauchamps

In fact, Richard's body was not buried until 1475. It was, as he requested in his will, placed in a chest in the south transept of St Mary's Warwick near to his parents' tomb – an elaborate canopied table with their effigies in brass, rather like a four-poster bed. Richard's son, Henry, became earl aged fourteen and, with the exception of the de Lisle estates which were inherited by his eldest step-sister Margaret from her mother Elizabeth, received the vast Beauchamp and Despenser estates and fortunes. The teenaged Henry was spending most of his time at the royal court, where he was receiving his education alongside his near-contemporary Henry VI. The Beauchamp line was, however, almost at its end for Henry, having recently been elevated to the rank of duke, died on 11 June 1446 before reaching the age of twenty. The estates passed via his sister Anne, the youngest of Richard's five children, to her husband Richard Neville, who became the new earl of Warwick and is popularly known as the 'Kingmaker'. On his death at Barnet in 1471 all Beauchamp rights passed to the Crown, the title and estates being held personally by Richard III and Henry VII. The fortune and influence built up by successive Beauchamp earls since 1268 was lost.

Richard's second wife Isabel died only a few months after her husband on 27 December 1439, and was buried in Tewkesbury Abbey. The executors and the five children had two tasks – to build the chapel requested in his will, and to oversee the estate. The chapel which they built on the south side of the chancel at St Mary's is remarkable for three reasons. Firstly, we possess an extensive set of records which give us insight into the costs, materials, designs and craftsmen involved in the project. Secondly, it presents us with the most complete example of late medieval craftsmanship in England. Metalwork, glass painting, woodwork, sculpture and of course architecture are all represented and are all of the highest quality. Thirdly, the chapel survived the Puritan period with very little damage and the main focus of interest, the tomb and effigy of Richard himself, were untouched.

The foundation stone of the chapel was laid in 1443, and the building and its decoration took twenty-one years to complete, at a cost of about £2,400, plus an additional £720 for the tomb. These figures are extraordinarily high, reflecting the standard of materials and craftsmanship. By comparison, the cost of the large Collegiate Church and almshouse built at Tattershall in Lincolnshire in the 1460s was £1,200 – less than half the cost of the Beauchamp Chapel. [35]

At the centre of the chapel is its *raison d'être*, Richard Beauchamp's life-size effigy, made of 'latten' (an alloy similar to bronze). It was cast by William Austen of London and covered in gold by Bartholomew Lambspring, 'a dutchman'. In this task they were assisted by Roger Webbe, a barber (presumably for his surgeon's knowledge of anatomy), and John Massingham, 'a kerver.' It is unlikely that the effigy is an accurate portrait. The armour is of a style first made in Milan more than a decade after Richard's death, and so could not have been his own.

Richard's head rests on a swan, part of the Beauchamp crest, which implies descent from the legendary Lohengrin. Under his right foot is the Beauchamp bear, and under his left the Despenser griffin. On the right hip of the effigy there was originally a dagger, present in an illustration of 1806 but now missing. Spurs were probably also attached, since there appear to be fixing holes, but there is no known illustration of these – they were certainly missing in 1806. Richard's hands are held in an attitude of prayer, open to allow him to gaze upon the figure of Mary, crowned Queen of Heaven, in the ceiling. That this is the only cast-metal effigy of a non-royal figure before the sixteenth century shows Richard's reputation. Over the figure of Richard is a 'hearse' – a cage-like construction built to support a fabric cover, tapestry or velvet, which would have been removed to reveal the effigy only when mass was said for his soul. There are only two other such hearses in the country – one over the figure of Robert, son of William the Conqueror in Gloucester Cathedral, and the other in the church at West Tanfield in North Yorkshire.

Around the sides of the Purbeck marble tomb, carved in Dorset by John Essex, are weepers representing mourners for his death, angels, and figures of the bear and ragged staffs. The angels and weepers – notable members of Richard's family and the nobility – were also cast by Austen. At the head of the tomb are representations of Richard's son, Henry, and Cecily Neville, Henry's wife, daughter of the earl of Salisbury. Cecily's brother, Richard Neville, 'the Kingmaker', is nearest to the altar on the south side of the tomb. Each of the weepers is identifiable from the enamelled coats of arms around the base. The inscription around the tomb, which is probably the first monumental eulogy written in the English language, punctuated by miniature bears and ragged staffs, reads :

> Prieth devoutly for the sowel whom God assoille of one of the moost worshipful knightes in his dayes of manhode and conning, Richard Beauchamp, late Eorl of Warrewik Lord Despenser of Bergevenney and of mony other grete lordships whos body resteth here under this tombe in a fulfeire vout of stone set on the bare rooch. The which visited with longe siknes in the castel of Roan therinne decessed ful christenly the last day of

april the yer of our Lord God A.D. MCCCCXXXIX he being at that tyme lieutenant genal and governer of the royalme of Fraunce and of the duchie of Normandie by sufficient autoritie of our sovaigne lord the king Harry VI. The which body with grete deliberacon and ful worshipful conduit bi see and by lond was broght to Warrewik the III day of October the yer above seide and was leide with ful soleime exequies in a feir chest made of stone in this churche afore the west dore of this chapel according to his last wille and testament therin to reste til this chaple by him devised in his lief were made. Al the whuch chapel founded on the rooch and alle membres therof his executors dede fully make and aparaille by the same auctorite the dide translate fful worshipfully the seide body into the voute aboveseide. Honorid be God therfore.

John Prudde, glazier to the king, undertook the glazing work, using Flemish glass – English glass was not considered of a sufficiently high quality – which cost 2s per square foot. By comparison, even the elaborate windows at Eton given by Henry VI cost only 1s 4d. The bottom half of the east window of the chapel is now a patchwork of original fragments left after puritan troops vandalized the chapel during the Cromwellian period. At the same time the reredos was smashed and the altar destroyed. (The present reredos is a replacement, designed by Timothy Lightoler in 1735.) Despite the damage, there are some sections of the window, perhaps as much as half, in their original positions. Four figures half way up the window, to the left and right of the central panels, are original and represent St Thomas of Canterbury, St Alban, St John of Bridlington and St Winifred, the patrons of the monastic houses to which Richard bequeathed gold statues of himself in his will. The other figures in the east window are reassembled fragments of Old Testament characters, including bits of the figures of Mary and Elizabeth. There is also a curious head of Christ, wearing a crown of thorns, which was probably originally from a crucifixion scene in one of the side windows.

In the centre of the window was the figure of Richard himself, kneeling in prayer. This was originally flanked by his two wives, Elizabeth and Isabel, and their five children. The head on the present central figure is clearly not Richard's – it probably belongs to one of his wives or daughters. The upper sections of the window, between the stone traceries, are almost in their original positions. The upper layer displays Richard's Despenser motto 'Louey Spencer tant que vivray' – 'Praise Spencer as long as I live' The next layer of lights down represents seraphs holding scrolls with the words and notes of 'Gloria in excelcis' (Glory to God in the highest).

On the north and south sides of the chapel, the windows would all have contained stained glass, but only that in the tracery now remains. The eastern sections contain a portrayal of a heavenly orchestra. This is of particular interest because the instruments which the angels play are excellent portrayals of mid-fifteenth century instruments, and are of considerable interest to students of musical history. The remaining tracery shows a choir of angels holding the music they are singing. This is a fifteenth century hymn to Mary, and it is sung in the chapel every year on St Mary's day (8 September).

The painted stone figures around the window are of at least as much interest as the glass itself. At the apex of the window is God seated upon a throne, surrounded by rays of glory and holding the world in the palm of his hand. Down the mullions and borders of the window are ranks of figures portraying the nine orders of angels –seraphim, cherubim, thrones, dominations, virtues, powers, principalities, angels and archangels. It is, however, impossible to decide which figures belong to which order. Some figures can be identified with a degree of certainty. One angel, who caries a sword and a tree, is the angel of the expulsion who stood guard at the gate of Eden to prevent Adam and Eve returning.

Also within the borders of the window are four saints: Barbara, with a tower in her right hand and a book in her left; Catherine of Alexandria carrying the sword by which she was martyred; Mary Magdalene carrying a pot of ointment, used to anoint Jesus; and Margaret of Antioch standing on the dragon which swallowed her. St Catherine and St Barbara were, of course, the two voices heard by Joan of Arc. Is there some reference to them here for that reason, or are they represented simply because they were popular in late medieval Europe?

It is tempting to read the chapel as an expression of Richard's personal Christian faith. He lies with a picture of hell painted on the west wall behind him, saints and angels in front and gazing at Mary crowned Queen of Heaven in the ceiling. This interpretation would be too convenient, however, and it is better to see the imagery of the building as a conventional expression of mid-fifteenth-century piety. Indeed, the concept of personally chosen faith would have been incomprehensible to someone of Richard's time. More than anything, the monument is a statement of social position; Richard's executors were making the point that he and his family were among the leading dynasties of Europe.

The chapel was ready by 1460, but Richard's body was not moved in until 1475. The reason seems to have been that his daughter Anne wished to delay the completion of the will. If she could hang on until her three half-sisters died, then the bequests to them would revert to her rather than being passed on to their offspring. At the service to dedicate the new chapel the bishop (presumably Worcester, in whose diocese Warwick then lay) sprinkled Richard's body with holy water. Then the remains were carried through the church while three Psalms were recited 'without note' (i.e. said rather than sung). As they reached the chapel, the remains were again sprinkled with water and the choir sang 'in paradisum' from the requiem mass. The following prayer was said by the bishop :

> We beseech your mercy Almighty, Eternal God who thought worthy to create man in your image and who wished the bones of your Saint

Joseph, son of Israel, to be brought to the promised land in exodus from Egypt, likewise for the soul of your servant Richard Beauchamp, today we transfer his bones to a new tomb. May you undertake to exercise your power for him, speedily and mercifully, that the darkness of darkness may not cover him, and that not for him be the shade of death. Absolve him of all his sins and collect him unto the bosom of Abraham, the place of rest, that he may rejoice so to be, so that when the day of judgement shall arrive his soul, with his heavenly body may be placed with your saints and elect forever, by Christ our Lord.

Following this prayer, holy water was sprinkled on the tomb, and Richard's remains placed within as antiphons were sung.

This might appear to be the end of the story. More than three decades after Richard's death his wishes have been completed and he has been laid to rest in one of the most magnificent buildings of the fifteenth century. However, two notable documents were to be produced in the next decade, each of them having Richard as the main focus. The first was The Pageants of Richard Beauchamp which, as suggested in chapter 2, it is most logical to assume was produced around the time of the transfer of his body into the chapel. The Pageants is unique as the only pictorial biography of the century of an individual historical figure – not even kings had such a fine biography to commemorate them. It is important to realize that the Pageants is primarily pictorial; the text clearly takes second place. The method of production seems to have been that the illustrator drew the plates in pencil, then went over them in brown ink. The text was then added. On some plates the text had to be squashed into the available space; on others too much space was left, and the text did not fill it. The work of the same illustrator has been detected in other late fifteenth century works, including a version of Ovid produced by Caxton and now in the Bodleian

---

LIV

Here shewes that howe Erle Richard hadde ij ladies the first hight Dame Elizabeth lady lyle by heneretaunce of her modre and she was doughter to the lorde Barkeley. by whom he hadde issu as appereth undre. And by his secund lady Dame Isabell late Countesse of Worcestre and heire to the lorde Spenser he hadde a son called henry heire to them both first Erle of Warrewik then by kyng henry the vjth made chief Erle of Englond and after Duke of Warrewyk. Also Erle Richard hadde by his ijde lady Dame Anne Countesse of Warrewik.

This genealogy obviously provides clues to the purpose of the Pageants, but it is puzzling why this and the one which follows are not complete. Richard and Elizabeth, on his right, have their arms fully drawn. Isabel's are only sketched in outline, and the five children have only blank shields on roundels.

LIV

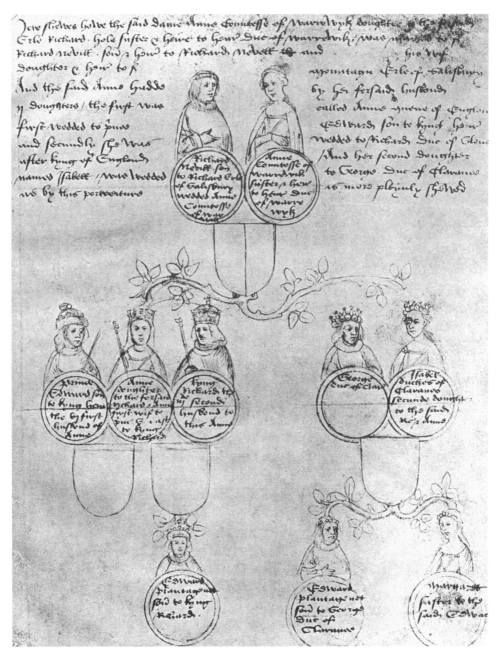

LV

LV

Here shewes howe the said dame Anne Countesse of Warrewyk doughter to the foreseid Erle Richard hole suster and heir to henry Duc of Warrewik was maryed to Sir Richard Nevill son dc heire to Richard Nevell and his wif doughter and heir to Sir Mountagu Erle of Salisbury. And the said Anne hadde by her forsaid husbon'd ij doughters. the first was called Anne quene of Englond first wedded to prince Edward son to Kyng henry and secundly she was wedded to Richard Duc of Glouc after Kyng of Englond And her second doughter named Isabell was wedded to George Duc of Clarance as by this portreiture is more pleynly shewed.

The second of the two genealogies concentrates only on Anne, Richard's fifth child. Her marriage to the 'kingmaker' is shown at the top of the chart, and their daughters' marriages below. None of the coats of arms are filled in, suggesting that the artist was unable to complete the work.

Library in Oxford. He has been described as 'one of the foremost artistic personalities of his time.'[36]

The main intention of the illustrations is clearly to portray Richard as a knight in the chivalrous tradition. Thus, for example, in a series of jousts in France, he appears on successive days in different coat of arms belonging to his ancestors, including Guy of Warwick, in what seems to be a deliberate echo of Arthurian legend and other romantic chivalrous deeds. It is somewhat ironic that Richard is portrayed as the paradigm of chivalry at precisely the time when such chivalry was becoming anachronistic.

The other document exists in two versions, and again the precise dating is uncertain. John Rous was a priest at the Chantry Chapel endowed by Richard at Guy's Cliffe, and was also an important fifteenth-century antiquary. Born near Warwick in about 1411 he wrote several histories, and although most of his works perished in the fire of Warwick of 1694 some, including the one known as the 'Rous Roll', still exist. This document, the English version of which is on seven joined pieces of vellum and is some 23ft long, gives brief biographies of kings of England, as well as the earls of Warwick and their families. Each brief text is illustrated with a line drawing of the person and a coloured coat of arms. In the English version the final section, dealing with Richard III, is a later addition and is written in a different script from the rest of the document. Again, this suggests that the roll was substantially completed before 1483 when Richard III became king, and his visit to Warwick in the summer of that year may help to date the final section of the roll.

In the past it was assumed that John Rous was the author of the Pageants as well as of the Roll, partly based on the view that two of the most significant literary figures of the fifteenth century were unlikely both to have been working in Warwick at the same time. The differences between the two works, however, makes common authorship improbable and the minor points of similarity (for instance, Richard is described as the 'father of courtesy' in both) are best explained either by Rous having access to the Pageant, or by both being based on first-hand information supplied by the family.

The section devoted to Richard is the longest in the roll. The illustration shows him holding the Beauchamp Chapel in one hand and the infant Henry VI, with orb, sceptre and crown, in the other. The interest of the biography is more local than national, and Richard is praised for his improvements to the town of Warwick, for his plans to make the Avon navigable and for his chivalrous deeds. A female seer, Emma Raughton of York, is cited as predicting that Guy's Cliffe would become a great religious foundation and place of pilgrimage, no doubt telling Richard what he wanted to hear. A mere four lines are given to national matters, briefly covering only his tutorship of Henry and his role in the two coronations.

Neither the Beauchamp Pageant nor the Rous Roll are reliable historical documents in the modern sense, and the interest of the former lies more in the quality of the illustrations than in the information conveyed. They are, however, significant in demonstrating the importance with which Richard was viewed four decades after his death, at a time when the Wars of the Roses were reaching a conclusion and England was moving rapidly out of the middle ages. The motivation behind their production may well have been his daughter's attempts to have her fortune restored, but this lessens neither the unique nature of the documents nor the magnitude of their central character.

Despite the continuing importance which attached to Richard in the fifteenth century with the building of the chapel and the production of two important documents, his world was quickly passing. Within two or three generation of his death, the medieval order, which had shown signs of cracking for a century, came to an end. The tensions over the succession of the monarchy that had dominated English politics since the death of Edward III in 1337 came to an end with the accession of Henry VII, and the Tudors were to bring a period of stability and economic growth. English claims to French territory, with the exception of Calais, became less important. The longbow, which had revolutionized war in the middle of the fourteenth century, was itself superseded by new technology. Books, once a rare luxury belonging only to the very rich, were printed and distributed widely. Most importantly, authority structures underwent a seismic shift. As the Reformation advanced, the Roman Church no longer held a grip on belief and behaviour. The power once assumed by magnates such as the Beauchamps was in decline and as the sixteenth century advanced, Parliament became more important as a moderating influence.

Richard Beauchamp was among the greatest English nobles of the Middle Ages; he was also one of the last great figures of chivalry.

Notes

1. Desmond Seward, *Henry V*, London, 1987, p.50
2. C.D. Ross, *The estates and Finances of Richard Beauchamp, Earl of Warwick*, Dugdale Occasional Papers, 1956
3. *The Oxford Illustrated History of Medieval England*, ed. Nigel Saul, Oxford, 1997, p.244.
4. Sebastian Barfield, *The Beauchamp Earls of Warwick 1268-1369*, University of Birmingham M.Phil. thesis
5. L. McGoldrick, *The Literary Manuscripts and Literary Patronage of the Beauchamp and Neville Families in the Late Middle Ages c. 1390 – 1500*, Newcastle Polytechnic Ph.D. thesis, 1985
6. Barfield, *op. cit.*
7. McGoldrick, *op. cit.*
8. McGoldrick, *op. cit.*
9. Alexandra Sinclair, *The Beauchamp Earls of Warwick in the Later Middle Ages*, London University Ph.D. Thesis, 1987
10. Sinclair, *op. cit.*, p.136
11. Seward, *op. cit.*, pp.51-2
12. Sinclair, *op. cit.*, p.105
13. Seward, *op. cit.*, p.117
14. Christopher Allmand, *Henry V*, London, 1992
15. Seward, *op. cit.*, pp.149-50
16. Sinclair, *op. cit.*, p.106
17. C.D. Ross, 'The Household Accounts of Elisabeth Berkeley, Countess of Warwick', *Transactions of the Bristol and Gloucester Archaeological Society*, 1951, pp.81-105
18. M. Keen, *English Society in the Later Middle Ages*, Harmondsworth, 1990
19. Christine Carpenter, 'The Beauchamp Affinity', *English Historical Review*, 1980
20. Seward, *op. cit.*, p.186
21. Sinclair, *op. cit.*, p.121.
22. Carpenter, *op. cit.*
23. Sinclair, *op. cit.*
24. B.P. Wolffe, *Henry VI*, London, 1981, p.51
25. R.A. Griffiths, *The Reign of King Henry VI*, Stroud, 1998
26. Quotations are from Jules Quicherat, *The Trial of Rehabilitation* and from Edward Lucie-Smith, *Joan of Arc*, London, 1976.
27. Marina Warner, *The Trial of Joan of Arc*, Evesham, 1996
28. D. Styles and C.T. Allmand, 'The Coronations of Henry VI', *History Today*, May 1982
29. Wolffe, *op. cit.*, p.61.
30. Griffiths, *op. cit.*, p.241.
31. K.B. McFarlane, *The Nobility of Later Medieval England*, Oxford, 1973, pp.197-200.
32. Carpenter, *op. cit.*
33. Griffiths, *op. cit.*, pp.199-206.
34. Sinclair, *op. cit.*, p.132.
35. Richard Marks, 'In Search of Abbot Thomas's Treasure', unpublished inaugural lecture at York University,
36. Kathleen Scott, *The Caxton Master and his Patrons*, Cambridge, 1976, p.62.

Bibliography

MANUSCRIPT SOURCES

British Library

Add. 16,164F 254.b Ballade made of Isabelle, Lady Despencer

Add. 17,228 Proposals made by Richard Beauchamp as Guardian of Henry VI to the Privy Council, 1432

Add. 24,194 The Trevisa Manuscript – Higdon's Polychronicon

Add. 28,564 Accounts of the executors of Richard Beauchamp for the building of the Lady Chapel in St Mary's Church, Warwick

Add. 32,091 f32 Prices of commodities 6HVI, taken out of a book of household expenses at Warwick Castle, 1427 – 1428

Add. 48, 976 The Rous Roll

Julius E IV The Beauchamp Pageants

Harl. MS6466, 35 – 36 (Description of the transfer of Beauchamp's body into the Beauchamp Chapel)

Lansdown 1 The Last Will and Testament of Richard Beauchamp

Warwick County Records Office

The Beauchamp Cartularly, 1100 – 1268

The Beauchamp Family Household Book

The Beauchamp Household Accounts, 1431 – 1432 (Transcribed by Marie-Veronique Cliu-Meyer)

PRINTED SOURCES

Allmand, C., *Henry V*, London, 1992

Barfield, S., *The Beauchamp Earls of Warwick, 1268-1369*, University of Birmingham M. Phil. Thesis, 1997

Bevan, B., *Henry IV*, New York, 1994

Bradbury, J., *The Medieval Siege*, London, 1992

Burne, A.H., *The Agincourt War*, London, 1991

Carpenter, C., 'The Beauchamp Affinity : A Story of Bastard Feudalism at Work', *English Historical Review*, Vol. 95, 1980

Cockayne, G.E., *The Complete Peerage*, 13 Vols, London 1910-1940

Connoly, M., *John Shirley : Book Production and the Noble Household in Fifteenth Century England*, London, 1998

Cronne, H.A., *The Borough of Warwick in the Middle Ages*, Dugdale Society Occasional Papers, 10

Cronne, H.A., and Hilton, R.H., 'The Beauchamp Household Book : Account of a Journey to Warwick in 1432', *University of Birmingham Historical Journal*, 1950, pp.208-18

Curry, A. and Hughes, M., *Arms, Armies and Fortifications in the Hundred Years War*, London, 1994

Dillon, Viscount, *Pageant of the Birth Life and Death of Richard Beauchamp, Earl of Warwick*, London, 1914

Douglas-Murray, J., *Joan of Arc*, London 1902

Dugdale, W., *Antiquities of Warwickshire*

Ferguson, A.B., *The Indian Summer of English Chivalry*, North Carolina, 1960

Given-Wilson, C., *The English Nobility in the Late Middle Ages*, London 1987

Glamorgan County History, Vol III

Goodman, A., *The Loyal Conspiracy: The Lords Appellant Under Richard II*, London, 1971

Gransden, A., *Historical Writing in England c. 1307 to the Early Sixteenth Century*, London, 1982

Griffiths, R.A., *The Reign of King Henry VI*, Stroud, 1998

Hutchinson, H.F., *The Hollow Crown, A Life of Richard II*, London, 1961

Keen, M., *Chivalry*, Yale, 1984

Keen, M., *Medieval Warfare*, Oxford, 1999

Kirby, J.L., *Henry IV of England*, London, 1970

Lander, J.R., *Conflict and Stability in Fifteenth Century England*, London, 1969

Lewis, P.S., *The Recovery of France in the Fifteenth Century*, London 1971

Lloyd, J.E., *Owen Glendower*, Oxford, 1931

Lucie-Smith, E., *Joan of Arc*, London, 1976

Marks, R., 'In Search of Abbot Thomas' Treasure', unpublished inaugural lecture, University of York

Marks, R. and Morgan, N., *The Golden Age of English Manuscript Painting*, London, 1981

McFarlane, K.B., *England in the Fifteenth Century*, London 1981

McFarlane, K.B., *The Nobility of Later Medieval England*, Oxford, 1972

MacCracken, H.N., ed., *The Minor Poems of John Lydgate*, Early English Texts Society, 1961

McGoldrick, L., *The Literary Manuscripts and Literary Patronage of the Beauchamp and Neville Families in the Late Middle Ages c. 1390-1500*, Newcastle Polytechnic Ph.D. Thesis, 1985

McNiven, P., 'The Problem of Henry IV's Health', *English Historical Review*, 1985, p.743 ff.

Privy Council Proceedings, 1428 – 1439

Pugh, R.B., ed., *Victoria County History of Warwickshire*, Vol. 8, London, 1969

Ross, C.D., *The Estates and Finances of Richard Beauchamp, Earl of Warwick*, Dugdale Society Occasional Papers, 12

Ross, C.D., *The Household Accounts of Elisabeth Berkeley, Countess of Warwick*, Bristol and Gloucester Archeological Society, 1951

Ross, C.D., *The Rouse Roll, With an Historical Introduction*, Gloucester, 1980

Scott, K.L., *The Caxton Master and his Patrons*, Cambridge, 1976

Seward, D., *Henry V*, London, 1987

Seward, D., *The Hundred Years War*, London, 1978

Sinclair, A., *The Beauchamp Earls of Warwick in the Later Middle Ages*, Ph. D. Thesis, London, 1987

Skidmore, I., *Owain Glyndwr: Prince of Wales*, London, 1978

Styles, D., *Financial Account of St Mary's Warwick, Michaelmas 1410 – Michaelmas 1411*, Dugdale Society Vol. XXXI

Styles, D. and Allmand, C.T., 'The Coronations of Henry VI', *History Today*, Vol. 32, May 1982

Tuck, J.A., *Richard II and the English Nobility*, London, 1973

Warner, M., *The Trial of Joan of Arc*, Evesham, 1996

Wolffe, B.P., *Henry VI*, London, 1981

Wright, C.E., 'The Rous Roll : The English Version', *British Museum Quarterly*, 1956

Wylie, J.H., *The Reign of Henry V*, Cambridge, 1914

Index